CALIFORNIA'S
BEST NATURE WALKS

CALIFORNIA'S BEST NATURE WALKS

32 EASY WAYS TO EXPLORE
THE GOLDEN STATE'S ECOLOGY

CHARLES HOOD

TIMBER PRESS + PORTLAND, OREGON

Frontispiece: This Giant Forest sequoia shows the red
bark and dense needles that give these giants their
world-famous color and shape.

Opposite: Forster's terns winter on the coast, breed in
the Bay Area, and migrate statewide.

Published in 2024 by Timber Press, Inc.,
a subsidiary of Workman Publishing Co., Inc.,
a subsidiary of Hachette Book Group, Inc.

1290 Avenue of the Americas
New York, New York 10104

timberpress.com

Printed in China on responsibly sourced paper
Text & cover design by Hillary Caudle
Illustrations by Shutterstock/arxihtu4ki and
Encyclopedia Britannica, 9th Edition.

The publisher is not responsible for websites (or their
content) that are not owned by the publisher.

The Hachette Speakers Bureau provides a wide
range of authors for speaking events. To find out
more, go to hachettespeakersbureau.com or email
HachetteSpeakers@hbgusa.com.

ISBN 978-1-64326-102-7

A catalog record for this book is available from the
Library of Congress.

CONTENTS

INTRODUCTION

California is America's America.

—SUSAN SONTAG

T hank you for joining me on this tour of California's most interesting, iconic, and (in some cases) most underappreciated natural sites. In these pages, we will visit the oldest trees in the world and also the tallest ones, and go from coastal Monterey, home to sea otters and sea urchins, to the shores of Mono Lake, a desert basin where the water is three times saltier than the ocean. We have endemic birds on offer, rare flowers, earthquake-loving fish, and ultra-cute island foxes. In the trips outlined here you can hike for five minutes, five hours, or five days. Some trips are a bit harder than others, but among the options here are sites that don't require much more than a hat and a good book—no trekking poles or cleated boots needed.

‹ Although it can snow in the high desert, most winter days are like this: clear, windless, and shirt-sleeve warm.

A Quick Look at the Numbers

When it comes to nature in California, some people are surprised at the numbers: 684 species of birds have been verified and 32 kinds of whale and dolphin. According to herpetologists, in California there are 160 reptiles and amphibians. In comparison, Great Britain only has 28 "herps," and that includes introduced species and some one-time-only sea turtles that probably will not occur again. Plants, too, are just as varied here, and the current list of endemics (that is, plant species found no other place in the world besides California) hovers around 2100—and that's not counting things like bristlecone pines, which are found here and in just a few other states. Meanwhile, once-rare species like bald eagles are making a resurgence and can be seen along the Pacific coast, in the pines at Lake Tahoe and Big Bear, and even along the Colorado River.

A fledgling kingbird says, "But Mom, I'm still hungry!" ▾

California Through the Seasons

Perhaps you have heard that tired cliché that California has no seasons. Balderdash! Horsefeathers! Every month something new is happening. In January, some owls are already nesting, and by mid-February, Costa's hummingbirds are migrating through the desert. March hillsides blaze lavender with blooming ceanothus. Midsummer in the High Sierra gives us crystalline blue skies and perfect green meadows. In fall, big-leaf maples turn as red as any tree in Vermont. And in midwinter, if things are snowed over in the high country, that is when the Salton Sea and Anza-Borrego are at their most ideal.

There is no bad time to explore nature. I recently stopped by Sacramento National Wildlife Refuge at what should have been the worst time to visit. It was midsummer in the middle of the day during a heat wave, and it was a heat wave during a drought year to boot. Conventional wisdom is that this refuge is best as a winter site (for geese flocks and otters and sandhill cranes), and if one does have to go out in summer, always start early, maybe even before dawn.

▲ A bald eagle waits out a spring storm near Big Bear.

But for me, I was not able to be here any earlier—I was driving down I–5 and it happened to be the middle of the day when I was passing by. Temperature at 11 a.m. was already 97 degrees. "This will be hopeless," I thought as I pulled onto the refuge's auto tour loop.

And yet it turned out to be a great day. Despite the heat and my pessimism, I saw deer and jackrabbits, swallows and gulls, plus herons, lizards, dragonflies, and turtles. Ibis flocks lifted up, bronze in the sun. At the lookout deck, a pair of western kingbirds fed their insistent young. Heat or no, I had to leave the windows down just to hear the thrum and buzz of an interconnected and fully "switched on" universe. I was glad I had stopped, and at the same time a bit embarrassed I had second-guessed the refuge in the first place.

Always give nature the benefit of the doubt.

▲ Fall colors light up Convict Lake in the Eastern Sierra.

How to Use This Book

This book lists sites north to south and also clockwise, so in section one, we start just north of San Francisco at Point Reyes, proceed up to the Oregon border to Lava Beds National Monument, and then swing back down to the Sacramento area. Then in other sections we go east to Tahoe and the Owens Valley, down to the middle of the state for sites in Monterey and Sequoia National Park, and finally move south to consider the coasts and deserts of Southern California.

This "clock" strategy allows us to tour a rich diversity of habits and ecosystems and also to encounter the many different stewards and agencies managing wild lands on behalf of the rest of us. All sites can be reached by a normal car on a normal weekend or vacation trip—no axle-breaking dirt roads, no overnight trails, and no map-and-compass route finding. Obsidian Dome (page 80) is the only exception; if you want to go to the best part, that is 3 miles up a rough-ish road. A regular SUV will be fine, but you need to go slowly and be careful. For lower cars, there's an option at the 1-mile mark that can be reached by anything other than a Lamborghini.

Even the Channel Islands (page 132) are right next to a road— or at least the departure dock is. Once you park, you need to take a one-hour boat ride to reach Santa Cruz Island. It's a great trip, and the channel as you cross over is one of the most reliable places in the world to see large pods of common dolphins. (I've spotted dolphins on ten of my past twelve crossings.)

Notes on Fire and Fire Ecology

There have always been wildland fires in California, either lightning-caused or intentionally set by Indigenous Americans. After these first inhabitants were harassed, killed, dispossessed, or dispersed, new Anglo-Europeans took over, and with them, new forest management practices were instituted. These turned out to be a bad idea, as fuel loads increased and non-native grasses filled in disturbed areas on the map.

In the end, a century of misapplied fire suppression resulted not in "no fires at all," but in "bad fires that can't be stopped." That is

A firefighter checks damage on a sequoia after 2021's KNP Complex Fire.

where we are now, pivoting to new management ideas. Drought and climate change only make previous patterns worse. Particularly in the past ten years, we have seen unnaturally large and hot fires, and we have seen the fire interval (how often things burn before they burn again) become increasingly brief.

You will see signs of recent fires in half the sites listed in this book. In Lava Beds National Monument (page 38), 70 percent of the park burned in 2020, and then in 2021 another 27 percent burned—97 percent of the park experienced big fires in just two years. As the historian Stephen Pyne suggests, our era should not be called the Anthropocene, but the "Pyrocene"—the age of fire.

With any hike in California, be aware of red flag warnings, and know that sooner or later a hike you really wanted to make may be off-limits for a month or two (or even a year or two) while crews assess fire damage and rebuild infrastructure. Prescribed burns, too, will become more normal going forward, and those cause temporary closures as well.

Even so, life carries on and nature will always survive, with or without us. If there's a single message this book wants to share, it's "Life finds a way."

"Hey, What About Place X?"

Your favorite place may not show up in these pages. Before you
send an angry email, know that some sites I wanted to include had
last-minute changes because of washed-out access roads or post-fire
closures. Other places are utterly fabulous but contain habitat similar
to a listed site, and so Arcata Marsh, for example, made the final cut,
while Orange County's San Joaquin Marsh did not.

With California, we have just too many good choices. Take sand
dunes for instance—Kelso Dunes in the Mojave National Preserve are
tall and otherworldly (see page 148), but Death Valley National Park
has many other potential dune sites, including the Eureka, Hidden,
Panamint, and Ibex dune complexes. It was hard to pick just one.

So, for now I wish you good days and happy trails, both in the
places described here and in the other great sites for which we could
not find room. Think of this book less as a ranked list and more as
an invitation to explore all the parks and canyons you've not been to
lately—or at all.

There are a lot of great pieces of ecology in California, and they
all await your next visit.

Let's lace up and get going.

Most sites in this
book welcome dogs,
but only if they are
on a leash. ▾

NORTHERN

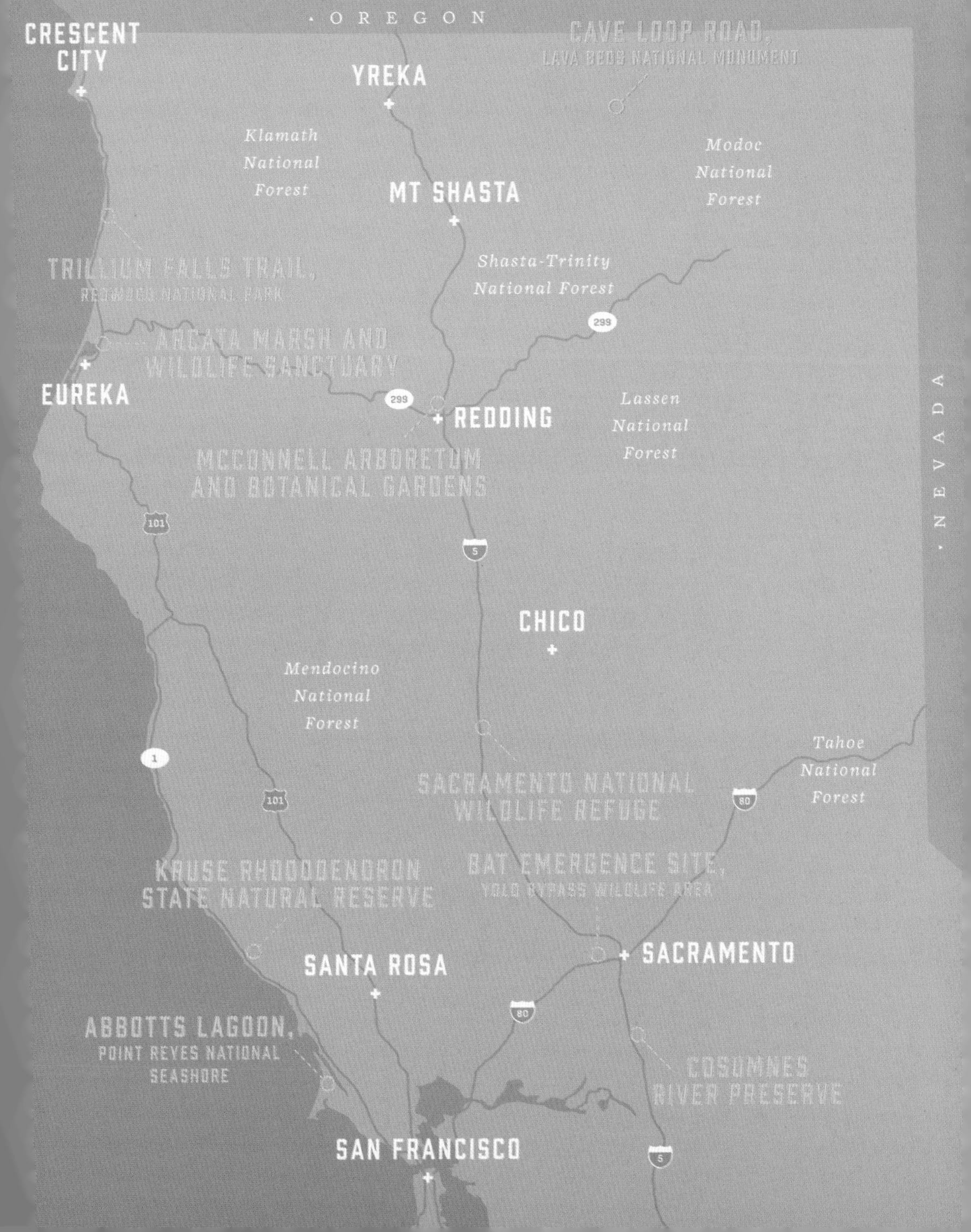

· O R E G O N ·

CRESCENT
CITY

CAVE LOOP ROAD,
LAVA BEDS NATIONAL MONUMENT

YREKA

*Klamath
National
Forest*

*Modoc
National
Forest*

MT SHASTA

*Shasta-Trinity
National Forest*

299

TRILLIUM FALLS TRAIL,
REDWOOD NATIONAL PARK

ARCATA MARSH AND
WILDLIFE SANCTUARY

299

EUREKA

REDDING

*Lassen
National
Forest*

MCCONNELL ARBORETUM
AND BOTANICAL GARDENS

101

5

CHICO

*Mendocino
National
Forest*

N E V A D A

1

*Tahoe
National
Forest*

101

80

SACRAMENTO NATIONAL
WILDLIFE REFUGE

KRUSE RHODODENDRON
STATE NATURAL RESERVE

BAT EMERGENCE SITE,
YOLO BYPASS WILDLIFE AREA

SANTA ROSA

SACRAMENTO

80

ABBOTTS LAGOON,
POINT REYES NATIONAL
SEASHORE

COSUMNES
RIVER PRESERVE

SAN FRANCISCO

5

ABBOTTS LAGOON
POINT REYES NATIONAL SEASHORE

Restored dunes and a chance to look for bobcats, otters, and rare shorebirds

DIFFICULTY
Moderate

LOCATION
Between Inverness and Pierce Point Ranch

LENGTH
3 miles

The bridge near the main lagoon sometimes offers close views of river otters.

Point Reyes is an hour and a half north of the Bay Area. It is a pleasant, scenic mix of historic dairy farms and coastal chaparral on a thin lozenge of land that the San Andreas Fault is trying to split off from the rest of California. As a park, it has more cool attractions than seems fair for one destination, including a dramatic fall elk rut, beaches carpeted with elephant seals, hiking and biking and horse-back trails, gray foxes to be looked for after dark, badgers that can be looked for during the day, bird-watching everywhere, and one of the most picturesque lighthouses on the West Coast.

The Abbotts Lagoon Trail leaves Pierce Point Road and wanders a level 1.4 miles west toward the sea, with the usual end being a bridge by a lagoon where river otters sometimes hang out. From the bridge, if you want to keep going, you can follow the dunes around the lagoon to keep heading toward the ocean. There is no set path at that point. Whether you go that far or not, by the bridge you should begin to hear the waves booming on the beach. If you walk past the bridge in summer, the southwest shoreline of lower Abbotts Lagoon is closed to access. This is to protect the nesting sites of the snowy plover, a small, endangered shorebird that looks like an all-white Easter chick. You can still get to the beach but cannot walk along the lagoon edge proper.

This hike is a good trail to do early in the morning. Walking out, you will have the sun at your back and if you're the first person to be hiking, the path and adjacent bushes will be busy with foraging quail, sparrows, brush rabbits, and maybe even a passing coyote or two. The real prize is to come across a bobcat. They are possible here, but the entire park is a good place to see bobcats, and especially in winter, when they hunt gophers during the daytime.

At its heart, this trail is about two things: hope and philosophy. Hope comes from all of the positive changes. In California, people like to go to the beach and to live at the beach, and because of that, our native dune ecology is almost gone, or else (if it remains), non-native plants crowd out native species. This site represents a restoration success story.

In the dunes past the bridge, non-native species such as European beachgrass and South African ice plant have been removed, and, in their place, restoration projects have brought back native plants, which in turn can sustain species like Myrtle's silver-spot butterfly. Despite its name, it is orange and black and found only in a few places along the Point Reyes and Sonoma coasts. In fact, thanks to restoration efforts, the dunes between the beach and the bridge support eleven federally listed plant and animal species.

Philosophy comes because much of the route from the trail-head to the bridge parallels grazed rangeland. This pastureland is Irish-green in spring, but note the absence of bushes or diversity, a reflection of the fact that this is a "mixed-use" park, not just a "pristine nature only" park. How do you feel about this overlap of goals? If you've ever had a milkshake or a cheeseburger, it's hard to criticize animal husbandry. Cows have to live *somewhere*, after all, and preserving historic ranching was one reason the park was established in the first place. Yet there is much controversy about land use patterns and where native elk here should or should not be allowed to go, and it seems each stakeholder is certain he or she is right while everybody else is part of a gang of chowderheads and reactionaries.

This book stays neutral on the elk-cattle-habitat divide, other than to say that almost all park service management plans, whether for here or Yellowstone or the arctic tundra

Bobcats are mid-sized, stubby-tailed cats that eat coots, ducks, rabbits, and gophers. ▾

⌃ Great blue herons are patient but relentless; this one hopes to catch a frog or a fish.

⌃ White-crowned sparrows can be tame and abundant along this trail.

in Alaska, include a period open to public commentary. I invite you to decide your position on mixed-use policies, and next time things come up for revision, to share your views. The only footnote I will add to the invitation is that it is always more complicated than it seems at first glance.

Yet once you flush a bobcat or get to make a video of frolicking otters, environmental impact reports and other documents will seem to belong to a galaxy long ago and far away. Nature as it is now will be enough, and that is true if you see only—"only," in air quotes—a great blue heron or a ground squirrel or a family of quail, and nothing more exotic.

As for the site name, grammarians agree: It really should be written as "Abbotts' Lagoon" (with a plural apostrophe), after the family of John Abbott, the nineteenth-century justice of the peace for Tomales Township. Of course, to take it to its logical conclusion, this location doesn't really need an Anglo-European name at all, but instead we could revert to the Native American titles that interpreted the California landscape not that long ago.

KRUSE RHODODENDRON STATE NATURAL RESERVE

A regrown redwood forest, home to rare flowers and a diverse mushroom array

DIFFICULTY
Easy

LOCATION
Between Stewarts Point and Fort Ross on Highway 1

LENGTH
.25 to 2 miles

This preserve is at its most spectacular in May, when the Pacific rhododendron (*Rhododendron macrophyllum*) blooms with large, pink, azalea-like blossoms. The Pacific rhododendron grows on the coast from British Columbia down through Washington and Oregon, ending more or less at this site (with a few records as far south as Santa Cruz). It is hard to overpraise this plant, which is the showiest flowering shrub in the forests of western North America. It also gives us a taste of Asia, since that side of the globe is the center for most rhododendron species. Further, in late winter and early spring, Kruse Preserve—named after a donor family—is a great place to hunt for mushrooms.

This hike makes our book for another reason, since it shows how enlightened management practices can restore degraded habitat. After being stewarded by the Kashaya Pomo for thousands of years, this part of the coast fell victim to the post–Gold Rush timber boom, with the original Native Americans dispossessed, and the tan oak and redwood taken out as fast as the whipsaws could cut and the San Francisco–bound schooners could be loaded. The opened-up

▲ The large, smooth leaves and showy pink blossoms of the Pacific rhododendron.

land then was used as pasture to raise sheep and cattle. Since then, the land has slowly been reforested, and visits today allow one to hike in the shade of coastal redwoods, Douglas firs, ferns, orchids, and red-barked madrones. It is an example of second-growth forest, but a well-managed second growth that feels as majestic and lush as primary woodland.

Best access to the preserve is from the northbound side of Highway 1, since you won't need to make a left turn against a busy lane of traffic. After you make the turn, the entrance road is unpaved, though it is not as rough as warning signs proclaim, and most cars should have no problem. Trails branch off from the access road—just pick one that looks intriguing (and has shaded parking); I recommend them all. The Chinese Gulch Trail connects with the Phillips Gulch Trail for a 2-mile loop, or equally satisfying is the short Rhododendron Loop Trail, not even a quarter of a mile long. The namesake plant species is the state flower of Washington; other names include rosebay and big-leaf rhododendron. The blossoms come out as early as March and usually last into mid-June.

Close by is Fort Ross, a state park and another example of contested landscape. It was established as a supply center for Russian fur traders who had come from Alaska and worked their way down the Pacific Coast with an entourage of enslaved Aleut hunters, planning to take every last sea otter they could spear or club. These pelts entered a global trade network, and sea otter fur from the Sonoma Coast could end up in markets as far away as London and China. Russia's Pacific colonies all ultimately failed, but this one lasted 30 years, from 1812 to 1842.

While Fort Ross was an imperialist outpost based on exploiting natural resources, it was also an example of a blended community, and a community which by necessity had to accept intermarriage and cross-cultural influences. In the early nineteenth century, inhabitants in this area included Russians, Alaskans, Kashaya Pomo, and mixed-race families of all the above. It is a time about which many present-day Californians do not know enough. The first windmills in California were built at Fort Ross, and California exports to fur-trading bases in Alaska included butter, apples, cherries, cabbage, pumpkins, and turnips. Russia being so close (and pushing so hard down the coast) made Spain nervous; one interpretation of the establishment of the northernmost missions is that it was a way for Spain (and later Mexico) to try to create a zone of influence that would block Russia's southward expansion.

Through all of this geopolitical wrangling, nature carried on and can be enjoyed today as an example of the

⊳ The banana slug is the largest land mollusk of North America. It can be 10 inches long.

⊳ Moist forest floors are ideal for mushroom-spotting. Some kinds are poisonous, so only eat the ones collected with experts.

⏶ This hermit thrush carries out its ablutions in the bed of a shallow stream. Frequent bathing cleans feathers and helps eliminate parasites.

adage "nature bats last." Listen, for example, for the ground-hopping, spot-breasted hermit thrush. It is robin-sized, with a russet tail. One guidebook explains that its "beautiful, haunting song begins with a sustained whistle and ends with softer, echo-like tones, described as *oh, holy holy, ah, purity purity eeh, sweetly sweetly*." Another birding reference describes the song as "ethereal [and] fluting."

All we know is that this bird makes a beautiful forest even more beautiful, and if the thrushes are singing *and* the rhododendrons are in bloom during your stopover, the trip review gets even more gold stars than usual.

ARCATA MARSH AND WILDLIFE SANCTUARY

An estuary wetlands complex with many trails, sloughs, ponds, and tidal edges

DIFFICULTY
Easy

LOCATION
Downtown Arcata near South G Street

LENGTH
.25 to 2 miles

In the 1970s, Arcata had to make a choice. No longer able to dump sewage directly into Humboldt Bay, residents had to envision alternate futures. They could build an expensive wastewater processing plant, such as most towns have, or they could try a bold experiment: What if they let nature passively do the filtration and treatment for them? Water slowly moving through reedbeds over months and years can come out as safe and purified as any outflow from a conventional sewage works, and, in fact, probably more safe and pure. And the marsh at the same time can provide habitat for wildlife. In restoring wetlands, Arcata would also be able to create new recreation opportunities, reclaim a disused sawmill, and become a model for other communities. That, in turn, would attract out-of-town bird-watchers (including this book's author), which would enhance tourism. Cliché but true: what a classic "win-win."

And so that is what they did.

The result is wildly successful. It now protects habitat but also attracts many user groups, from runners cranking out the miles to casual walkers pushing baby strollers. Numbers verify both quality of habitat and number of daily visitors. That is because many birders post sightings to an online repository called eBird, and the collective eBird list for Arcata Marsh and Wildlife Sanctuary currently rests at

This greater yellow-legs has just made a lucky catch. ▸

a whopping 341 species—more than for any single, one-stop site in this book.

That bird total will likely continue to rise as even more out-of-range strays become identified. Previous "oh wow" Arcata birds have included ducks and finches from Europe, ocean birds from the Pacific, and lost warblers from the American South. Some migrant birds get their internal compass points reversed, and instead of migrating to the Atlantic Coast and following that down to South America, they end up crossing the continent the wrong way and coming to California instead, where they push up against the Pacific Ocean. "Wait a minute," they say. "This doesn't look right *at all*." Expert spotters notice these stray birds and can document them for science and for their personal lists. Sometimes the wanderer finds the new area perfectly satisfactory, and it may return many winters in a row.

Which birds can be seen here? Ducks and herons and grebes and reed-lovers like the marsh wren and the common yellowthroat. Crows and hawks and peregrine falcons. Killdeer and sandpipers and mud-probing dowitchers, whose busy heads bob up and down

The main nature center overlooks a
slough that often hosts egrets.

like sewing machines finishing hems. Winter has the most species and the greatest numbers, though what one sees on any given morning depends on how foggy it is and if the tide is in or out on the adjacent mudflats.

⌃ River otters can be seen anywhere in the marsh. Signs warn, "Otter Crossing." Take it slow driving in.

Besides birding, this is also one of three "good for otter-spotting" sites in this book. The first was Abbotts Lagoon (page 18) and the other is Sacramento Wildlife Refuge (page 47). River otters eat fish, frogs, turtles, crabs, and crayfish (or in your family, do you say "crawdads"?), but other, even bigger items are possible targets. At Abbotts Lagoon, at least some otters have become adroit at catching and eating brown pelicans, which they hunt from below. Here in Arcata, using the same "snatch and drag," ducks and coots are among the prey items that river otters take. If you see an otter and can take a picture, there's a community science project that tracks Humboldt's otters, and it has more than 7,000 records so far. Doing a search on social media for "HSU River Otter Citizen Science Project" should get you to the right place.

Other inhabitants here include raccoons, gray foxes, and many, many dragonflies. Spiderwebs accumulate morning dew and create their own kind of magical art.

"We're going to need a bigger coat"—a spiderweb shows nicely against a black background.

Most first-time visitors start at the interpretive center, 569 South G Street. You can park there, get a map, and follow any trail that catches your fancy—sooner or later they all will connect up and loop back. This is a terrain of intention and history, with layers that reveal prior use. Some local features reflect that in names like "Mount Trashmore" (former land-fill) and "No-Name Pond" (named by a professor on a whim, and now codified on official maps). I always find the staff at the Center to be friendly and knowledgeable, but if you arrive before it opens, maps and checklists are available online.

Another option is to take I Street along the edge of the mudflats and park at the road's end at Klopp Lake. If it's low tide, those black stumps stretching out into the bay are pilings from Arcata Wharf. Built in 1855, the wharf and horse-drawn railroad ran 2 miles into the bay.

You may want to go around with an expert, and several options present them-selves. Redwood Region Audubon Society and Friends of the Arcata Marsh (FOAM) both offer guided walks, and, if set up in advance, docents can escort school groups. It is worth joining them. After all, Arcata bird species number 342 may be only a binocular scan away.

Pink (or "red flowering") currant produces a berry that humans don't like but birds certainly do.

TRILLIUM FALLS TRAIL

REDWOOD NATIONAL PARK

A loop trail that includes old-growth forest, maples and alders, and a small but attractive waterfall

DIFFICULTY
Moderate

LOCATION
Highway 101 near Elk Meadow Day Use Area, 3 miles north of Orick

LENGTH
3 miles

This trail has a bit of everything: a bit of elevation gain and loss, a bit of logging history, a bit of a water feature at the small waterfall, and a bit of a crowd on warm weekends. Depending where you are on the trail, you might also hear a bit of traffic noise from Highway 101. Driving to the trailhead (which is just off 101), you pass an open area that, with a bit of luck, might give you good opportunities for photographing elk.

The route is named for a lily, the Pacific trillium, which was first collected for western science by Lewis and Clark in 1806, though of course Native Americans had known it for 10,000 years. As the photo on page 36 shows, it has three long white petals and a yellow center. Trillium can bloom as early as February and as late as June, but April is peak time. The petals fade to pink later in the season.

The parking lot marks the site of a former sawmill, but nearby a remnant patch of uncut forest allows this trail to work its way through large trees and relatively undisturbed understory. Besides coastal redwoods, there are bay trees and maples here, and enough fallen logs and young trees mixed in with tall, mature ones to give you a true sense of being in a living forest.

The "falls" are not much taller than a toddler, but they are attractive nevertheless. ▸

The falls of the trail's name are modest and quickly reached—would one call them a small cascade? A floodlet? A gurgling rush of stream-hop? Take your photos from the bridge, please, and don't try to go off the trail to get closer. This area sees a lot of visitors, and the off-trail traffic is detrimental to new plants and compacts the soil, which hastens runoff and damages roots.

About half of visitors turn back once they get to the falls, and that's fine—in this book, I encourage you to go out for as long or as short as feels best.

Continuing on lets you get into the general rhythm of a walk in the woods. Sometimes the forest is a bit thicker and closed in, sometimes there are sudden surprises like black mushrooms or the namesake trillium, and then suddenly one is back under the larger, taller trees again. There are huckleberries, blackberries, and especially ferns, oh so many ferns. Do not expect to see deer or even many squirrels; this site is about botany and the meditative act of walking more than it is about

▲ A hiker pauses to photograph a bird at the start of the Trillium Falls Trail.

Wherever soil accumulates (even 10 feet off the ground), plants thrive. ▸

active wildlife. The final section of trail takes you out of redwoods and back under alders as you return to the parking area.

This route is one of dozens of well-marked trails in Redwood National Park, also known as Redwood National and State Parks (RNSP), though the "state parks" umbrella includes three different sub-parks: Del Norte Coast, Jedediah Smith, and Prairie Creek. The collective reach of the four federal and state units protects about half of the old-growth coastal redwoods in the entire world. Somewhere inside RNSP, in what is supposed to be an undisclosed location, is the tallest known living tree, the Hyperion redwood, crowning out at

‹ The trillium is an attractive plant, and it glows bright white in the dim light of the understory.

a towering 380 feet. That means it is about 28 stories tall, one third of the Empire State Building. Few secrets are ever truly secret, and Hyperion's location is known to some, even if the Park Service will fine you for trying to go there. I very firmly believe in the "let it be" vote on this one and say that just knowing it is there is enough, and also that seeing so many other 300-plus-foot trees in the park feels perfectly satisfying. Craning your neck up, can you really tell a 300-foot tree from 310-foot one?

All redwoods face a challenge of physics, which is how one gets water from the roots to the top of the tree. That is a long way up just to rely on the capillary action of evaporation at the top to help siphon up water from the bottom. One answer is fog. In a coastal redwood, the top needles absorb water from summer fog and share that with the rest of the tree in a reverse flow, top down. (Fog also condenses on the trees' needles and drips to the ground as a low-grade but important rainfall.) Water movement limits vertical growth, but so does wind shear: The taller the tree, the more surface area gets exposed to wind, plus the more chance there is to be struck by lightning. And at ground level, the harder it will be to create roots deep and stable enough to anchor all that verticality firmly into the duff and loam.

Will an even taller redwood than Hyperion be found some day? Never say never, and on the Olympic Peninsula in Washington some monster specimens of Douglas fir were found in 2021, setting new records. (The tallest tree *ever* may have been a Douglas fir cut down in 1930.) So it is certainly possible, though if there *is* a 400-foot redwood out there, that location will be kept even more secret than Hyperion's is supposed to be.

In terms of longevity, coastal redwoods can pass 2,000 years, the giant sequoia trees of the High Sierra (page 104) can pass 3,000 years, and bristlecone pines (page 88) go past 5,000 years. We can admire a large, spreading oak, but it's still just a baby compared to these long-enduring and stoic witnesses.

CAVE LOOP ROAD
LAVA BEDS NATIONAL MONUMENT

Lava tube caves allow everybody in the family to take a turn as head explorer

DIFFICULTY
Moderate

LOCATION
Cave Loop is a paved road near the Visitor Center, halfway between the park's north and south entrances

LENGTH
.25 to 3 miles

Lava Beds National Monument lets us all become "spelunker for a day," as lava tubes provide a chance for kids of all ages to run (and crawl) with flashlights and discover what is behind the next bend. Aboveground, the rugged landscape is classic American West, with far vistas, a distant snow-covered volcano (Mount Shasta), and the remains of camps from the 1872 Modoc War, when the United States Army tried to eradicate the Indigenous Modoc, who were resisting dislocation from their ancestral lands. The park today includes 800 caves, ranked from beginner to advanced, though a few of these are closed to entry during summer in order to protect maternal bat colonies.

• Each person in the family should have her or his own light (and bring a spare, just in case).

Some bats are solitary, but Townsend's big-eared bats form nursery colonies. Lava Beds is an important maternity site for this endangered species. •

The Cave Loop is a paved road that provides access to thirteen caves concentrated in a radius of just a few miles. Check in with the rangers at the visitor center to get a free cave permit before setting out, learn about the protocols to protect bats from white-nose syndrome (a serious fungal infection decimating bats in the east), and check for updates on any closures or restrictions.

Most of the lava of Lava Beds dates from 30,000 to 40,000 years ago, with some flows twice as old and some as recent as only the past thousand years. Geologists use words from the Hawaiian language to describe types of lava; *pahoehoe* is smooth or folded into

ropes, while *'a'ā* is rough, sharp, and jagged. Lava tube caves form when the surface crust of molten lava cools but the interior is still flowing. When the eruption ends, interior lava drains away, leaving a hollow space that can be so big you could park an RV inside it.

The park also preserves Native American heritage,

including rock art at Petroglyph Point, on the edge of what used to be the ancient shore of Tule Lake.

▲ Juniper trees and lava scree mark the rugged landscape of this unworldly park.

If you're not sure that being underground is the right choice for you, an easy introduction starts with Mushpot Cave. It is the only cave in the park to have lights and interpretive signs. Ready to fly solo? Try Sunshine Cave, named for a break in the roof that not only lets light in but allows plants to thrive as well. You still need a flashlight to navigate the route to the break and past it. This is "out and back"; return the way you came in.

Everybody ready? Entrance ladder to enter Sunshine Cave. ▸

Fourteen species of bats live in Lava Beds. My favorite is the pallid bat, creamy tan in color and whose food includes beetles, crickets, centipedes, and scorpions, which it plucks right off the ground.

To hunt, it quarters back and forth slowly, 3–8 feet off the ground, similar to how a short-eared owl or northern harrier flies.

More typical are the habits of the Mexican free-tailed bat, which hunts mosquitoes and moths acrobatically in midair, using its radar-like echolocation. It can fly at over 100 miles an hour, a speed and agility which help when it migrates away in winter. Townsend's big-eared bats have huge ears; if you were this species, your ears would stick up 2.5 feet tall. On the plus side, you could hear what mean things people are saying about you at a party, even if you were in another room.

The park is open in winter, though snow closes some roads, and of course the bats are hibernating or will have flown south. The caves will still be here, though—next year and for many thousands of years to come.

MCCONNELL ARBORETUM AND BOTANICAL GARDENS

A river-adjacent plant walk, to learn flowers and see summer butterflies

DIFFICULTY
Easy

LOCATION
Downtown Redding by the north side of the Sacramento River

LENGTH
.5 miles

M any of us have heard the term "blended families," where adults and children from more than one relationship join into a new, often more dynamic, diverse family group. The focus of this site extends a related idea, that of "blended nature." Here in Redding, and indeed in almost every town or habitat we live in, multiple ecologies come together in each neighborhood to form a new "super" ecology, which is a mix of native and non-native species.

McConnell Arboretum focuses on plants that handle drought and heat well, which is to say plants that react well to the general California experience. In the garden, an appealing blend of plants from California and around the world combines to help make this corner of the city a calmer, more beautiful place. You will not find lush ferns or hothouses full of tropical orchids, but you *will* find birds and butterflies and native trees like the western redbud, a modestly sized tree whose dense bouquets of pink flowers in spring make it the happy equal to any cherry tree in Japan.

In thinking about what one could install instead of a traditional water-guzzling lawn, a good plant to learn about is deergrass, *Muhlenbergia rigens*, which requires little to no irrigation in the dry season. If you're looking for something native to plant that is drought tolerant and visually striking, one guidebook calls this plant "tidy and well-behaved." Deer do eat deergrass, but generally only when it is a young plant; mature stalks are tough and durable and can be used for basket-making. This is a prime location to see it, since (according to one garden manager) they have more California deergrass at McConnell than anywhere else in the world.

‹ Oaks, cotton-woods, willows, and sunshine—the perfect recipe for a spring afternoon.

Santiago Calatrava's Sundial Bridge links the gardens to other cultural sites across the river. ▾

Besides deergrass, deer are wild here but quite used to people and can be seen anywhere on the grounds. They look tame but are not; do not get too close doing selfies. What keeps the deer from eating the garden's flowers down to bare roots? It's a complicated story, one that was reviewed in the journal *Pacific Horticulture*. "Generations of deer raised in the gardens have been unfazed by motion-activated sprinklers. Fawns with water streaming off their coats found the *Alstroemeria* beds especially delectable. Applications of Liquid Fence, while effective, proved unpleasant for human visitors who didn't appreciate the rotten egg aroma. Deer Off is currently the preferred repellant and is sprayed on sensitive plants every two weeks."

What can we say? Managing nature is complicated. Even if denied their favorite flowers, the deer find plenty of other food,

▴ These California poppies are growing wild on a forgotten edge of the arboretum.

New World, Old World: A native pipevine swallowtail feeds on English lavender.

Carpenter bees look scary but won't sting you. They will, however, steal nectar by drilling a hole in the base of the blossom.

and they must be glad that inside city limits there will never be a hunting season.

Another animal to watch for here is the western gray squirrel, which is bushy-tailed and gray-bodied, with a white belly and a fierce gaze—at least it seems fierce if you get near any of its cached acorns or walnuts. Tree-dwelling squirrels like this one make a messy leaf nest called a drey. Another native rodent is the California ground squirrel. It sometimes goes up a few feet into bushes to be on the lookout or to reach a tender leaf, but it is mostly a ground-dweller. Less bushy-tailed than a gray squirrel, the ground squirrel is dun-brown with pale speckles.

Why do drab and brown when you can have electric blue with orange spots? Butterflies are abundant here from early spring to late fall. Besides the pipevine swallowtail shown in the photograph, others to watch for include cabbage white, fiery skipper, Lorquin's admiral, and silvery blue. (A "blue" is a kind of butterfly in this case, not just a color.)

Who provides plants their astounding common names? Some of the delights found here will give your mouth an explosion of aural and verbal texture when you say the names aloud, including spurge, vetch, sedge, stinkhorn, smokebush, sneezeweed, and my favorite: sticky mouse-ear chickweed. How can you identify all these? Both download-for-free and it-costs-money plant apps can give your botanical knowledge a big boost. You take a picture with your phone, confer with the app, and see what the cyber experts have to say.

About half the plants on-site are, as expected, water-thrifty native species like valley oak and manzanita, and half come from everywhere else, including South Africa, Chile, and New Zealand. Depending on where you live, your neighborhood trees probably show a similar ratio. In most of California, bird populations are a similar blend of origin stories: Malibu, Bakersfield, and San Francisco have feral parrots; Los Angeles has the munia and Swinhoe's white-eye, both from Asia, and the pin-tailed whydah of Africa. Everybody knows pigeons, North America's earliest introduced bird, originally table fare sold as "squab." We live in a time of movement and translocation, and like it or not, the nature around us is going to reflect that in its variety and its willingness to adopt and to adapt.

SACRAMENTO NATIONAL WILDLIFE REFUGE

Geese, ducks, otters—this auto tour route circles a winter wetland wonderland

DIFFICULTY
Easy

LENGTH
.25 miles

LOCATION
Off of I–5, south of Willows

You come to this wildlife refuge in winter to see approximately *one zillion* geese; you come in summer to see ibis and dragonflies, deer and turtles; and you come anytime just to get out of the city and have some wide views of sky and pond and nature and all things that are *not* about work, hurrying, or stress. As mentioned in the introduction (page 11), even visiting at the worst time of day on the worst day of the year—midday in summer during a heatwave during a drought—still ended up providing a really great day out in nature. As this book goes to press, the main reserve headquarters are being rebuilt; this site may well have a large, new interpretation center in the future, but for now the one-way-loop of the auto route is self-guided.

Where did the winter geese (and ducks and sandhill cranes) all come from? Broadly speaking, Alaska, but different species nest in different habitats, and some ducks and grebes nest at the refuge itself. The highest waterfowl counts happen in winter, though, as migrants pour down the Pacific Flyway.

Greater white-fronted geese graze in the foreground, backed by a white carpet of snow geese. ▾

An observation deck on the auto route allows visitors to get out of the car and scan the horizon.

Surveying this refuge and several adjacent ones, a recent census tallied four million ducks and one and a quarter million geese. This last category includes five goose species: snow, Ross's, Canada, cackling, and white-fronted. Besides these five core species, there are usually a few hybrids found each year, and onesies and twosies of strays and rarities, such as the emperor goose from Alaska, or a coastal species called the brant.

▲ A Wilson's snipe pauses in the open, its back displaying the cryptic pattern of its camouflage.

This refuge is also a chance to gain a small window into the past. Historically, the Central Valley was one big duck festival top to bottom, though most of the marshes were later drained for agriculture or to control flooding and protect cities like Fresno, Modesto, Davis, and Sacramento. This preserve has many once-rare, now-recovering species, including river otters and beavers. One part of the original ecosystem that is still missing is a wetland-affiliated species called the tule elk. They would have been abundant here until the 1860s. Habitat loss and overhunting nearly made this elk extinct, but in the twentieth century the population partially recovered, and today you can see tule elk at Point Reyes (page 18) and Wind Wolves near Bakersfield (page 124). The elk at Redwood National Park are the same general species as tule and Rocky Mountain elk but represent a different subspecies, Roosevelt elk.

The United States Fish and Wildlife Service (USFWS) is in charge of this and all federal wildlife refuges, and we will meet them again at the end of the book, in Death Valley and at the Salton Sea. USFWS manages more than 500 refuges, protecting 150 million acres of habitat from the Aleutians to the Florida Keys. The agency's origins started in the nineteenth century as a fishery service and slowly evolved to include waterfowl hunting as well. That means this is a mixed-use refuge. During duck season, you want to remember when hunt days occur (usually Wednesdays, weekends, and holidays, from the end of October to end of January). There are also days set aside just for youth hunting and for veterans to hunt. Wildfowl populations are well monitored, and in California, all hunting—even falconry—is regulated. No matter how you feel about it as an outdoor sport, the reality is that hunting is part of American culture and supporting it is part of the USFWS mission.

Not surprisingly, the geese understand which days are hunt days, and since they have wings and know how to use them, they just go elsewhere those days. They can shift over to foraging at night inside the refuge itself or graze in gun-free zones adjacent to I-5.

By keeping land from being developed, wildlife refuges protect all species, game birds or not, so if you like marsh wrens, sandpipers, garter snakes, and dragonflies, be glad that the federal refuge system exists.

This is a good site for western pond turtles. This species can be hard to find in more urban wetlands due to competition from introduced red-eared sliders, the common pet trade turtle. ▸

BAT EMERGENCE SITE

YOLO BYPASS WILDLIFE AREA

In summer, thousands of bats leave crevices under a bridge and fly up in an awe-inspiring spiral

DIFFICULTY
Easy

LOCATION
East of Davis where Chiles Road meets the levee

LENGTH
.25 miles

A cloud of bats rises like smoke. Often peregrine falcons dive through, trying to catch a bat snack for dinner.

Bring a chair, bring a cooler, bring binoculars—this is roadside nature at its most convenient and most social. Along I–80 between Davis and Sacramento, up to 250,000 Mexican free-tailed bats emerge at dusk. They start slowly, banking and circling under the bridge itself, and then it's time. Using whatever bat cues bats use, suddenly more and more pour out into the open air, forming a funnel cloud of bats, all of them swirling up into the sky. Some clever person named these nightly occurrences "batnadoes." The bats gain altitude out of sight before dispersing to hunt individually over the surrounding marshland and rice fields.

That is not the only drama playing out. As the exodus reaches its peak, the black arrow of a diving peregrine falcon suddenly cuts through the main column. This species of bat, though, is a fast flyer, and has good eyesight and echolocation; the bats can dodge and twist, so the peregrine misses more often than not. You may see an owl give it a try as well. There is no fee to watch the bats here and no organized viewing platform; just pick a summer night and come on down to the Davis side of the bridge, making new friends or saying hi to old ones.

Many misconceptions linger, so time to do some fact-checking. First, no matter what the clichés say, bats do not spread rabies—or no more so than raccoons, cats, skunks, or Fido the dog. (If you come across a bat jerking on the ground and foaming at the mouth, please do not pick it up.) Yes, there is a species that laps up blood, and it is indeed called the vampire bat, but it does not live in North America. It occurs only in Central and South

A close-up view of a Mexican free-tailed bat. It can fly 100 miles an hour. ▾

America, and unless you are a somnolent cow bedded down in a pasture adjacent to a forest, you have nothing to worry about. Bats don't get in your hair, bats are not icky, and bats are certainly not mice with wings, even though their name in German is *fledermaus*.

Bats do, however, eat crop pests, and do so by the metric ton. Bats are the only mammal that can fly (not just glide), and worldwide there are 1,400 species, from small to large, found from deserts to swamps to mountaintops. Some bats eat frogs, fish, or fruit, but most, like the free-tailed bats here in Davis, eat insects. One bat can catch up to 1,000 mosquitoes an hour, which makes me wonder, "Can I rent one next time I go camping?"

The causeway has gaps built into it that are just right for a bat to tuck itself into. Meanwhile, the adjacent floodplain offers clear flying and good hunting, especially around the organic rice crops, where no pesticides can be used. The Yolo Bypass Wildlife Area starts here, where the causeway meets the high ground. It is an 8,000-acre sanctuary and agriculture area that is simultaneously a flood control

◂ I–80 crosses wetlands on this causeway that is home to 250,000 bats.

▴ Before setting out to hunt, bats swirl and mingle under the bridge itself.

basin, a set of productive ranches and farms, and a wildlife-dense wetland. It is also "bat heaven" after dark.

The primary species present at the bridge is the Mexican free-tailed bat (the same one you can see at Carlsbad Caverns in New Mexico and at Bracken Cave in Texas), which at twenty million is the largest known bat colony in the world. This species flies fast and high—up to 10,000 feet—and migrates to Mexico during winter. Some guidebooks name this the Brazilian free-tailed bat after its Latin name, *Tadarida brasiliensis.* The nonprofit Yolo Basin Foundation gives bat talks and bat tours, and sometimes they have captive bats they bring to these outreach events, if you ever wanted to see a live bat up close. These captives are bats that were injured and now cannot be returned to the wild. And no, their handlers do not have to chase around with butterfly nets trying to catch moths and mosquitoes at feeding time. A captive bat quickly learns to eat pet store mealworms held out by tweezers, and most seem content to be fed these all night long.

COSUMNES RIVER PRESERVE

An intact floodplain and riparian forest, plus an upland habitat for cranes in winter

DIFFICULTY
Easy

LOCATION
North of Thornton, south of Franklin, near I–5

LENGTH
.5 to 2 miles

"Run wild, run free" is a goal (and catchy slogan) for river restorationists everywhere. As a model, they look to the Cosumnes River, which is one of the only west-of-Sierra rivers that remains undammed and which still has (at least at this site) an intact and extensive river gallery forest. It was spared development not out of altruism but just because it was too minor to modify extensively, or at least it is minor compared to the American River and other Sacramento Delta waterways. (One historian calls it "the river that got away.") The river's headwaters are in the Sierra, and downstream from the preserve the Cosumnes flows into the Mokelumne, which later joins the collective drainage of the Sacramento–San Joaquin Delta. The word "Cosumnes" first entered European cartography in 1841, and does not come from Spanish. It probably originated from a misheard or mistranslated Miwok village name.

The main parking area and interpretive center are on Franklin Boulevard, and most trails leave from there. North of that starting point is a half-mile round-trip ADA-compliant boardwalk trail, reached from a smaller parking area. The main parking area allows access to the Lost Slough Wetlands and River Walk trails, and if one connected all the links and did every section of trail, a nice hike (or jog) of 4-plus miles can be worked out. If the day is hot or energy is lacking, a mile or less gives a good taste of features and habitats. The trail map is available online and at the visitor center, though to be honest, things are well enough signposted that you can just follow your nose and go wander, and still end up fine. If the main parking lot is locked early in the morning, there's informal tolerance of people parking on the street and walking in.

What should you look for? Anything and everything. Great trees here—cottonwoods, for example, one of which the staff guesses is 18 feet "dbh" (diameter at breast height). Flowers in spring. Birdsong year-round. Bald eagles nest here, and everybody likes them—or everybody does except for ospreys, whose fish the eagles pirate. Winter brings ducks, geese, and also up to 1,200 sandhill cranes, tall

‹ Water levels fluctuate depending on tidal influences and how much rain has fallen recently. At times this passage is fully flooded.

⌃ Sandhill cranes come here in winter
and are always exciting to spot.

◂ Most of Sacramento looked like this . . .
once upon a time. Cosumnes preserves
a lost world.

birds that are red-capped, gray-bodied, and
bustle-butted. They look like a great blue
heron wearing a Wilma Flintstone skirt.
Wingspan of 6 feet. Look for cranes in
flooded fields anywhere near the core of
the preserve, but not in forests or wooded
sloughs. Early December to late February
are the best dates.

When hiking, do be aware there is a lot
of poison oak around, so stay on the trails.

This preserve defies the odds in many
ways, including its complicated owner-
ship structure. Can plural relationships

◂ A swallowtail butterfly rests on a buttonwillow's floral "ball."

ever work smoothly? It seems to do so here, since this 50,000-acre reserve is managed by seven land-owning agencies. They include The Nature Conservancy, the Bureau of Land Management, California Department of Fish and Wildlife, Sacramento County Regional Parks, Department of Water Resources, Ducks Unlimited, and the California State Lands Commission. That list seems like it creates a dance with too many partners, but it works out to our benefit, since this open space is as popular with weekend hikers and back-slough boaters as it is with hawks, herons, ducks, and otters.

Fun fact: Even though this preserve is south of Sacramento and many hours from the Golden Gate Bridge by car, it is still part of the Pacific Ocean, since high and low tides (hours late and mostly attenuated this far inland) cause the local water levels to rise and fall each day. And since the earth's tides themselves are linked to the moon, you could truthfully say that the water levels are tied to a commanding presence not a hundred miles distant, but 229,700 miles away.

EASTERN

DONNER SUMMIT
CANYON

+ RENO

*Lassen
National
Forest*

*Plumas
National
Forest*

HICO

*Tahoe
National
Forest*

Lake Tahoe

+ CARSON CITY

N E V A D A

SACRAMENTO

*Eldorado
National Forest*

TAYLOR MARSH,
LAKE TAHOE BASIN MANAGEMENT UNIT

TUFA SPIRES,
MONO BASIN NATIONAL SCENIC AREA,
INYO NATIONAL FOREST

*Stanislaus
National Forest*

OBSIDIAN DOME,
INYO NATIONAL FOREST

STOCKTON

CONVICT LAKE,
INYO NATIONAL FOREST

OLMSTED POINT,
YOSEMITE NATIONAL PARK

MERCED

SCHULMAN GROVE OF
BRISTLECONE PINES,
INYO NATIONAL FOREST

*Inyo
National
Forest*

FRESNO

*Death Valley
National Park*

FOSSIL FALLS

BADWATER AND
PUPFISH SITES,
DEATH VALLEY
NATIONAL PARK

RIDGECREST +

BAKERSFIELD

SANTA BARBARA

DONNER SUMMIT CANYON

A historic trail that goes to a picnic site overlooking Donner Lake

DIFFICULTY
Moderate

LOCATION
Near Donner Lake past South Shore Drive, where Donner Pass Road becomes Donner Summit Road

LENGTH
3 miles

P art of lands managed by the Truckee Donner Land Trust, this route goes from the Donner Canyon trailhead to a scenic overlook called the Kathy Polucha Kessler Memorial Picnic Area. (Try saying that three times fast.) The really cool thing is that in addition to beauty and getting to traverse a former beaver pond, when hiking this trail you intersect five major layers of human history at once. The oldest foundation would be the Native American trade routes that crossed the Sierra here. Then came pioneer footpaths, then a wagon road, and after that the first auto route in the area, a road called the Lincoln Highway. Once it came through, the train would no longer be the only way to cross the country; this was the first transcontinental road in the United States intended for automobiles, dedicated in 1913. The era of the road trip had begun.

The crimson columbine blooms from April into late summer. ▾

In time, a better and wider grade was needed to handle the flow of traffic. When the Lincoln Highway was rerouted, the abandoned road became a trail once again. Yet where you are hiking still remains an important if invisible transportation corridor. That is because miles of fiber-optic cable are buried underground, connecting

The trail follows the historic route of the Lincoln Highway, opened in 1913. ▸

Reno to the rest of the Pacific Rim. On this trail you are walking under spruce and cedar, but on top of billions of pulses of data.

Route-finding is straightforward. From the trailhead, drop into the drainage, cross the bridge, and follow the signs to Donner Summit Canyon. You're going to stay on the main trail as it goes through forest and meadow, crosses a stream, and begins to gain elevation. A signposted side trail bends back the way you have come to pass Dave's Bench and ends with granite slabs, picnic tables, and an inspiring view of Donner Lake. This is the Kathy Polucha Kessler Memorial Picnic Area. You're above 6,000 feet in elevation here, so don't be shy about taking it slowly and stopping to catch your breath (and update your social media feed). Car to vista point

↑ Even if you don't observe western gray squirrels directly, gnawed cones on the side of the trail reveal their presence.

◄ This former beaver pond is on its way to becoming a meadow.

is a mile and a half, making this out-and-back 3 miles round trip.

Given how pretty the hike is and the visitor pressure in the Tahoe area overall, this is a surprisingly under-visited trail. Horses, dogs, mountain bikes, and long-distance runners are all welcome; in winter, you can do this route on snowshoes.

The "Donner" of the name means the Donner Party, a group of settlers caught near here without appropriate supplies in the winter of 1846–47. Some died, some did not, and the most neutral thing to say is that (passive voice) decisions were made—not all of them rational or wise, but the people involved did what they felt was necessary to survive. The Donner Party's story and that of Native Americans of the region is well-told inside the museum and visitor center at Donner Memorial State Park. This is 2 miles from the trailhead, closer to downtown Truckee. Deserved or not, there is a very large, heroic pioneer memorial there as well.

Look here for western gray squirrels, large and gray and bushy-tailed, and also the smaller Douglas squirrel, a more mixed gray and brown up top and creamy orange underneath. They are always active it seems, and always hungry. "Nature is mouths," writes Joyce Carol Oates. "Or maybe a single mouth." She means what the Victorians would have said is "nature red in tooth and claw," with each thing trying to hunt the next thing.

A classic example of this can be seen in individuals of the genus *Laphria*, the bee-mimic robber flies. Watch for them here in summer. This is a large fly that looks like a regular bee but has a thicker waist. Looking like a bee is good camouflage, so their potential victims do not suspect the big zap about to come. Other insects think, "Oh, just a bee, they eat flowers, nothing for me to worry about." This fly, though, hunts a variety of insects (including other robber flies), using its proboscis to penetrate the prey insect's body. Once attached, it injects enzymes to dissolve the victim's tissue.

Sometimes the fiercest predators are the most easily overlooked.

TAYLOR MARSH
LAKE TAHOE BASIN MANAGEMENT UNIT

Hike through Jeffrey pines to a lakeshore
marsh with bald eagles and grand views

DIFFICULTY
Easy

LOCATION
Three miles north of South Lake Tahoe, on the east side
of Highway 89, near Tallac Historic Site

LENGTH
1.5 miles,
route-dependent

A short walk through the forest brings you
to this spectacular view of Taylor Marsh.

Lake Tahoe is famous—and famously crowded. And yet despite the crowds, fires, weekend traffic, trash-addicted black bears, and jaw-dropping real estate prices, Lake Tahoe endures, and it only takes one visit to see why it remains so popular. The color of the water is one; the lake is 1,600 feet deep (second only to Crater Lake in the Lower 48), and in some light looks a deep, crystalline sapphire. The range of recreation is another, from mountain bikes to dogsleds to snowboarding. There are lots of ways to "do" Lake Tahoe, and of the many, many choices, this featured site is all about "wow," not subtlety. If you were only going to do one hike in all of the Tahoe Basin, it should be this one (and be sure to bring your camera).

Your starting point is the Taylor Creek Visitor Center. The mega trees in the parking lot are champion examples of never-been-logged Jeffrey pines, which is a species common throughout the Tahoe area. In theory its bark smells like vanilla, butterscotch, and/or almonds, but how strongly you experience that depends on the individual tree and how acute your imagination (I mean your sense of smell) is.

When done smooshing your face into the bark crevices, take the Lake of the Sky Trail past the amphitheater north to the water's edge. This forested first half mile offers Sierra flowers such as woolly mule's

The snow plant is a root parasite: pretty, red flowers rise above ground, but the plant itself is out of view. ▾

ear, which has a pale, fuzzy-looking vertical leaf that does look a bit like a mule's ear, if mules were sage green and grew out of the ground. Part of the aster family, it produces long-petaled yellow flowers with yellow centers, which are pollinated by bees and other insects.

You reach the lakeshore at Kiva Beach. Walking left lets you get closer to Taylor Marsh proper, though there may be barriers in place for plant restoration. Beavers live here, upstream and usually out of

◂ Chipmunks are small, active squirrels with racing stripes from nose to tail.

◂ Bold and curious, Steller's jays are all blue with a peaked cap.

sight, and restoration efforts include tarping the bottom of creeks to shade out Eurasian watermilfoil, an invasive aquatic plant that displaces and reduces native aquatic plant diversity. The *konk-a-ree* calls from the marsh come from red-winged blackbirds, while *scrill-screee, scrill-screee* reveals an agitated killdeer.

Kiva is a classic "beachgoer's beach," popular with dogs and dog owners, and anybody who loves to wade and splash. A walk further northwest brings you to Baldwin Beach, another attractive destination. The white-and-black hawks soaring overhead will all be ospreys; their super sharp talons and grippy feet pads are designed to keep fish from escaping, once caught. Bald eagles are present as well, another fish-catching large raptor. Both male and female adults have the familiar brown body and white head, which ends in a huge, hooked, yellow beak. You often see Canada geese here, and the small terns over the water in summer are Forster's terns, named after Johann Reinhold Forster. He traveled with Captain Cook in 1776, and one dictionary of biology says that he was "unpleasant and troublesome to the end." The bird, though, is nice—acrobatic and white, with a forked tail and black cap.

Once done with the marsh and the splashy pleasures of Kiva Beach, a short walk east along the shore takes you to the pseudo-rustic, envy-inducing Tallac Historic Site, an enclave of waterfront estates dating from 1890 to 1920. This was the collective summer retreat for San Francisco's socially elite families, since then as now, money *does* buy happiness—or at least it buys really nice places to live. Twenty buildings are still extant, open for self-guided or docent-led tours. Taking a slow mosey around the site, it's hard not to say aloud, "Yes, I think I could have lived here quite happily, thank you very much."

The forest remains close at hand. Even directly around the houses you can hear and see birds, including nuthatches, jays, robins, and white-headed woodpeckers. Most ignore people and will let you get good pictures with even a modest telephoto lens. This all is nature that is easy to appreciate and parking-lot adjacent; assuming no forest fires are nearby, breathing deeply seems a particular gift here. To quote Mark Twain, "The air up [here] in the clouds is very pure and fine . . . . And why shouldn't it be?—it is the same air the angels breathe."

TUFA SPIRES

MONO BASIN NATIONAL SCENIC AREA, INYO NATIONAL FOREST

Photogenic rock spires rise out of the famous lake surrounded by alpine and Great Basin scenery

DIFFICULTY
Easy

LOCATION
By Lee Vining on Highway 395

LENGTH
1 mile

n California, most rain arrives in winter, barreling in on giant
Pacific storms that flow west to east. The Sierra Nevada blocks and
alters those storm flows, so the Western Sierra is typically greener
and more forested, while the Eastern Sierra, hidden in the so-called
"rain shadow," is starker, dryer, and, thanks to geology, often more
vertical. This results in a landscape that is unique and highly photogenic, with an open sagebrush valley along Highway 395 juxtaposed
against the steep verticality of sheer mountains, sometimes spanning
10,000 feet of elevation gain in one sweeping vista. Winter or summer, the views are equally stupendous, and these views have inspired
photographers ranging from Ansel Adams to Galen Rowell.

Yet out of all the surreal beauty of the Eastern Sierra, the most
surreal site of all is the spire-ringed blue donut that is Mono Lake.
In a landscape that has low rainfall and where all water is allocated
(and usually over-allocated), Mono Lake improbably offers the
visual illusion of being a gift of the greatest treasure of all—water . . .
trillions of gallons of fresh, pure water. But a walk along its crunchy,
tufa-crumbling shoreline, as the harmless black flies swarm every

‹ Postcards do not
lie: The tufa spires
create dramatic
foregrounds for
Mono Lake photo-
graphs.

A solo kayaker
ventures into the
main lake. If you do
this, be careful of
afternoon winds. ›

◂ The entire region offers great vistas; turning away from the shore and looking south gives this expansive view. Recently, herds of wild mustangs have been seen here.

◂ Snow adds visual contrast to a classic Mono Lake scene.

footstep, allows one to touch and taste the truth. To dip a finger into the lake it to be surprised by three things. One is that the water is cold, the next is that it feels slimy, and the last (lifting finger to lips) is how bitter it tastes.

The mechanism behind this is simple. Water flows into Mono Lake, but the only way out is through evaporation, and as the water evaporates, salt and other elements stay behind, becoming more and more concentrated in the remaining basin. (We will experience this at the Salton Sea as well.) This process is sped up thanks to Los Angeles's Department of Water and Power, which diverts incoming streams as part of how they deliver water to L.A. That means Mono Lake is three times saltier than the ocean and getting a tiny bit saltier each year. It also means that the lake water, to be fully honest, tastes like gym socks soaked in baking soda.

The tufa spires are a result of the same minerals that help create that chalky taste. When the water level was higher, underwater springs released calcium-rich outflow into carbonate-rich lake water. This formed limestone around the mouth of each spring. Over time, these deposits layered higher and higher. When Mono Lake's water level receded, the improbable towers were left behind on dry land, looking a bit like plaster knockoffs of a show cave's best stalagmites.

To see the spires, the usual hike is the South Tufa Loop Trail, reached by following the signs on Highway 395. Kayaks and canoes can launch from nearby Navy Beach. Less visited are the parts of the western shore reached north of Lee Vining from the Picnic Grounds Road spur. And for bird watching, it's always worth having a look at Mono Lake County Park off of Cemetery Road. There are restrooms here, a boardwalk down to the shore, and a mix of lawns and trees that attract everything from sapsuckers to flycatchers to pocket gophers.

The lake itself (or rather, islands in it) provides a nesting site for 50,000

▲ More than 50,000 California gulls nest at Mono Lake. They mostly feed on brine flies.

California gulls, while more than a million eared grebes stage up on the lake in fall, feasting on brine shrimp and alkali flies before migrating on to wintering grounds farther south. Phalaropes, sandpipers, geese, pelicans, and ducks all stop at Mono Lake as well. The swallows around the tufa spires can be several species, but most expected is the violet-green swallow.

Legal challenges from Friends of Mono Lake and other organizations have resulted in rulings intended to keep water diversions from draining Mono Lake down to a sticky puddle of salty mud. While DWP legally has to live up to these mandates, there is no judge in the world who can make a megadrought comply with desired outcomes.

OLMSTED POINT

YOSEMITE NATIONAL PARK

An unusual view of Half Dome and a hands-on experience with the "left-behinds" of glaciers

DIFFICULTY
Easy

LENGTH
.25 to .5 miles

LOCATION
Tioga Pass Road, between Porcupine Flat Campground and Tenaya Lake

Completed in 1961, the current Tioga Pass Road probably should never have been built. Ansel Adams opposed it, and due to the heavy snowpack, the Park Service closes it seven months out of the year, since it is too high and wild to plow easily.

The road (also called Highway 120) connects Yosemite Valley to Lee Vining, Mono Lake, and the Eastern Sierra, cresting out at Tioga Pass just shy of 10,000 feet. No matter whether the decision to build the current alignment was right or wrong, now that the modern road is here, most visitors are glad to have it. Tioga Pass Road allows swift access to the glacier-scoured bare rock of the Yosemite high country in ways that a back-packing or horse-packing trip would take many days to match. And this, indeed, is high country at its most glorious, with granite domes, exquisite meadows, and one of the nicest lakes (Tenaya Lake) in the entire National Park system.

Situated at 8,418 feet, Olmsted Point is not the highest point on the road, but it does have great views in all

Nearby Tenaya Lake is also a popular stop. ▾

directions. This is all granite slab country; so little soil has had a chance to accumulate that the terrain is mostly bare rock. You can see the top of Half Dome from here, and you can see cute little hamster things called pikas, but most importantly, you can see the scrub and haul of the Ice Age's great glaciers.

At the height of successive ice ages, an ice cap 2,000 feet deep covered the Tuolumne Meadows region and what is now the Tioga Pass Road. One portion of this ice cap flowed in a 45-mile-long glacier down what is now the Tuolumne River gorge. Other glaciers pushed into nearby canyons, and following Tenaya Creek, one glacier made it all the way into Yosemite Valley. These slow but inexorable rivers of ice helped round over granite domes, move boulders the size

◂ Granite and trees populate an "only the essentials" view of Yosemite high country.

▴ A lone tree has found a crack in the granite.

of a two-story house, and sheared off the fronts of immense cliffs, such as happened with the face of Half Dome.

The ice came, it stayed for thousands of years, and in time it retreated. The meltwater helped fill inland seas, a remnant of which is now Mono Lake. As they pushed and pulled themselves back and forth across the landscape, these glaciers left visible marks of their passage. Some geologists call this part of Yosemite an open-air classroom, since the rock here now tells the story of these titanic past events. There are many processes on display here. Let's start with glacial polish.

The term "glacial polish" applies to granite that has been wiped clean by moving glaciers, leaving sections with a shine or patina finish, often located on the upcanyon side of a dome or rocky slope. Sections are usually discontinuous—there will be a big slab that is cleanly and continuously polished; then, due to exfoliation or erosion, there is a rougher patch; and then the polished part resumes. Sometimes you need to be looking at an oblique angle (rather than

straight on) to see it most clearly. Afternoon light can help, rather than direct noon sunlight.

Specialists call a secondary version of this process "subglacial water polish," which is glacial polish that appears fluted or sculpted and was formed by water flowing long ago beneath the main mass of a glacier.

"Erratic" can mean a bad driver or an impetuous personality, but add "glacial" to "erratic" and the word pair denotes "a free-standing (and often huge) boulder left behind when an ice sheet retreats," according to one reference. One of the best places in California to see textbook "glacial erratics" is here at Olmsted Point. Erratics are literally stranded boulders, immense rocks moved from many miles away and now isolated on a granite slab,

▲ If your phone or camera has a black-and-white mode, Olmsted Point is a good place to try it out.

The cute pika harvests meadow grass in summer and caches it for winter. ▸

most too heavy to move or slide ever again, even in the strongest earthquake or iciest winter storm. In odd ways, they are almost a kind of random art installation, and if you crouch or shift perspective, you can create interesting camera compositions with these house-sized rocks silhouetted against the sky.

No trails recommended or needed here: To see erratics and glacial polish (and other features, like exfoliation), park at Olmsted Point, cross the road, and then climb on the uphill rock slabs in any direction you want to go. It's safe and fun and you can't get lost.

The site name honors Frederick Law Olmsted Jr., a landscape architect who worked on a number of national park projects, including Tioga Pass Road. His father, Olmsted Senior, founded the then-new discipline of landscape architecture and also designed Central Park in New York.

OBSIDIAN DOME

INYO NATIONAL FOREST

A crater in the pine woods covered by obsidian, a black volcanic glass traded throughout California

DIFFICULTY
Easy

LOCATION
Off Highway 395 between June Lake and the Crestview Rest Area

LENGTH
.25 to 1.5 miles

W hat is harder than glass, sharper than a scalpel, and often ends up far, far from home? If you have seen this chapter's title, you know the answer. Obsidian is magma that cooled so fast it didn't form crystals, and so it is, quite literally, volcanic glass. If worked with a shaping stone, it shatters with scallop-shaped divots, and those can meet on both sides of a potential blade to create ultrasharp (if a bit irregular) edges. You have to know what you're doing, of course, but in skilled hands an obsidian blank makes extremely good arrowheads, scrapers, and spearpoints, and so has been coveted and traded for a long, long time. New research shows that hominins were working obsidian as far back as 1.2 million years ago.

Near Highway 395, on the edge of a former volcano, entire mountainsides shine with raw obsidian, and there's no access fee or restriction on visiting (other than the rough road to get there, per below). There is pumice here, too, which is another, lighter, more gas-filled kind of lava, and hybrid blocks that are a swirly mix of both materials: part pumice, part obsidian, like Neapolitan ice cream that has melted and frozen, melted and frozen.

‹ An obsidian boulder the size of a sofa glistens in the sun.

This well-worked obsidian point is in the National Park Service's collection at Point Reyes. ▾

The sheer quantity of obsidian is deeply impressive, and you have four options for seeing it yourself. Turn west off Highway 395 onto Obsidian Dome Road. The rocky slopes are directly adjacent to this dirt road. There are four places you can stop: the 1-mile mark, the 1.5-mile-mark, the 2.5-mile mark, and the 3-mile mark. The first two places are easy to get to in any kind of car other than the lowest of low sports cars. Both of those stops will let you hike around one main deposit. There is a second, better location, but to get there the road is narrow and rocky enough that

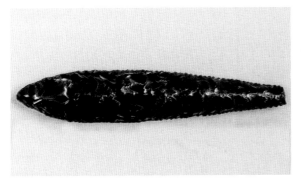

a light truck or SUV might be a good choice. In a small car, if you are slow and careful, you can go as far as the 2.5-mile mark, park there, then walk the final half mile. Higher clearance vehicles should have no trouble. (As always, use common sense.)

▴ A short drive from Highway 395 brings you to a wall of obsidian blocks.

The reason to go to the second site is quality: The better obsidian slope is deeper into the forest but has finer rocks. It is worth the effort. Of course, if you have mountain bikes you can park anywhere and sail along. On a bike you can also pick up side trails that go north and south to June Lake and Mammoth Mountain.

When visiting these deposits, you are standing at the center of a radius of tradition and wealth. A map of pre-contact trading routes looks like a plan for the interstates and cross-Sierra highways today. Native Americans traded fish, tobacco, baskets, textiles, feathers, beads, obsidian, and horses and guns, later on. There are no tribes that did not participate. The Achomawi, for example, traded salmon and tule baskets with the Northern Paiute in exchange for bows and shell beads. The Cahuilla, located in what is now Riverside, received gourd rattles from the Yuma on the Colorado River and basketry from the Chemehuevi, near present Lake Havasu. The Central Miwok supplied shells and glass beads to the Mono tribes, and the Mono furnished them with ocher paint and rabbit-skin blankets. There are the bones of macaws in New Mexico middens, and shells from the Pacific Ocean have turned up in Oklahoma. That means that obsidian from this trip's scree slopes might end up as a spearpoint many hundreds of miles away.

Obsidian continues its slow global circulation today. A search of the British Museum database turns up 500 entries for obsidian tools, amulets, mirrors, and arrowheads—none of which originated in the British Isles. In Los Angeles, the Autry Museum's archive lists a thousand obsidian entries. At the same time, museums are never static. Museums loan items, deaccession items, reevaluate and re-catalog items, and (rarely) repatriate objects to their home cultures. An obsidian arrowhead in London today may be in Mexico City tomorrow.

Obsidian is usually black, but other forms are possible, including red, brown, gold, gray, and green. It depends which impurities got mixed in. Some rockhounds want to collect all the colors, leading unscrupulous dealers to try and pass off substitutes—not volcanic glass but bottle glass, sanded and artificially weathered. I promise you that at this site, everything is real and authentic, from the bottom of the scree slope to the top of the pines.

Jeffrey pines around the site support varied wildlife, including this western tanager. ▸

CONVICT LAKE

INYO NATIONAL FOREST

Fall colors, grand views, and popular fishing in a glacier-carved basin make this a "best of" for the Eastern Sierra

DIFFICULTY
Easy

LOCATION
Off Highway 395 between Mammoth and Crowley Lake

LENGTH
.5 to 2.5 miles

We first met this site in the autumn foliage photography on pages 12–13. And while it is glorious in fall, most visitors come in summer, and many of them want to fish.

We are at 7,850 feet here, with cool mornings and warm (even hot) afternoons. The road ends in a "T" at the main outlet of the lake, with parking in both directions. Fishing options include walking the shore, bringing or renting a boat, or working the stream below the lake.

In all three cases, most people are after one thing: trout. The native species in the Sierra (and California's state freshwater fish), the golden trout, never occurred this far north. Instead, introduced rainbow trout now dominate the water. The resident population gets a periodic boost from the California Department of Fish and Wildlife, which restocks the lake with hatchery-raised fingerlings. From there they just keep growing, unless a passing osprey or random black bear intervenes. One very skilled or very lucky person caught an 11.5-pound trout here in 2022—in photos, it looks as big as a salmon—and that record-setter had been preceded by a 10-pound rainbow the month before.

For solitude (and easier parking), try visiting in winter.

A "fish-eye" view of a rainbow trout, the most commonly stocked species. ▾

Convict Lake can be reached by tanker truck, which is how its fish arrive. Yet higher lakes in the Sierra are stocked by Cal Fish and

Wildlife as well. Formerly all the fish for the backcountry were delivered in tall jugs strapped to the backs of pack mules. That is slow and of course limits how many fish you can provide per trip. Now, aircraft pour them right out of the sky, with an approach and release as precise as any World War II bomb run.

While rainbow trout is the main species, brook trout

and brown trout also live here. Any fisherperson worth her or his creel will know this already, but the fishing season starts on the last Saturday of April, one hour before sunrise, and it ends on November 15, one hour after sunset.

△ Calm mornings create "picture postcard" photo ops.

Hikers, fishermen, and bird-watchers share the same trail to circumnavigate the lake, which takes 2.5 miles start to end. Wear a hat: most of the route is not shaded, so in summer it gets hot. Opinion is evenly split if it is more scenic to go clockwise or counterclockwise from the parking lot at the bottom of the lake, and in this book, I remain agnostic on the question. Mule deer, chipmunks, golden-mantled ground squirrels, California quail, robins, and mountain bluebirds are all common at the trailhead and on the hike.

Golden-mantled ground squirrels look like chipmunks but are larger and have orange heads. *

Two mountains overlook Convict Lake. Closer and more obvious, Laurel Mountain (11,818 feet) is made of metamorphic rock, not granite, which gives its sheer face a mix of swirls and banding not present in places like Olmsted Point. Also visible is Mount Morrison (12,241 feet). It is named after Robert Morrison, who was killed in 1876 while guiding a posse that was chasing convicts who had escaped from a penitentiary in Nevada. Another member of the posse, a Native American named Mono Jim, also died in the shootout; he, too, has a summit named in his memory.

As for the six fugitives after whom the lake is now named, two were taken to Bishop and hanged, three were sent back to Nevada, and one got away.

SCHULMAN GROVE OF BRISTLECONE PINES

INYO NATIONAL FOREST

A 1-mile loop trail traverses the oldest trees on the planet, with a bonus track of marmots and bluebirds

DIFFICULTY
Moderate

LOCATION
From Westgard Pass on Highway 168, go north on White Mountain Road 10 miles to the visitor center

LENGTH
1 mile

This bristlecone pine may be 4,000 years old (or even older).

I n March 1958, *National Geographic* published a startling article. There were trees, it reported, that were more than 4,000 years old. They grew in a desolate mountain range east of the High Sierra called the White Mountains. Nobody expected this; previously the oldest trees were thought to be sequoias, a thousand years younger. The article's author was Edmund Shulman, a tree expert who had discovered their true age, and for whom the forest is named now.

Since his work, even more ancient bristlecones have been found, including claims—sometimes disputed—of specimens that may be older than 5,000 years. Sticking to certified consensus, the top age of a living specimen is the Methuselah Tree, 4,854 years old as we go to press. Happy birthday, survivor, though you may yet be outranked. Not that many bristlecones have been accurately surveyed, so older ones are almost certainly still out there. It may take us 50 years, but we're likely to find them. Age is verified by checking a core sample against a tree ring database that now spans 10,000 years.

These are the world's oldest non-clonal organisms, meaning a single, continuously growing plant that is not a clone of itself. They're surprisingly easy to see; you can reach them in an hour's drive from Bishop, taking paved (albeit narrow and windy) roads. Our recommended hike is the Discovery Loop Trail, 1 mile round-trip, but we hasten to add that you don't need to take the trail to see bristlecone pines—good examples start right at the visitor center. If you do take the trail, it includes benches, and since you're above 10,000 feet here (the highest site in the book), don't be shy about using them. It takes a few days to acclimate, so if you're feeling the altitude, go slowly and drink lots of water. Longer trails are possible as well.

Not all the trees here are as old as Methuselah. Some are babies, only 1,000 or 2,000 years old. Even so, that is twice or ten times the age of most oaks. What allows these trees to live so long? Eight things come together in their favor. One is the soil, which is a kind of limestone that is too harsh for most other plants. That leaves more snowmelt for the bristlecones and also prevents underbrush from

Few things can live
in this limestone soil,
but a bristlecone
can. Being isolated
from other trees
helps protect it from
wildfires.

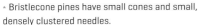
⁂ Bristlecone pines have small cones and small, densely clustered needles.

⁂ A yellow-bellied marmot takes in the sunset.

accumulating. That means wildfires are rare and localized. Another is their wood, which is dense and resin-filled and hence highly insect-resistant. And at this altitude—9,000 to 11,000 feet (the main bristlecone "zone")—there are not many insects to begin with. Third, in such a harsh world, they do not have any other major plants trying to compete with them for light and nutrients, and very little wants to eat them. Even porcupines don't often wander this high.

Fourth, the habitat is so high and cold, harsh and windswept, that it is a terrible place to be a fungus, which makes it a very good place to be a tree. In fact, fallen wood does not rot, but instead slowly erodes away like a fallen statue or a relic from a Roman ruin.

Fifth, dormancy. Having a bad year, a bad decade? The tree grows so slowly it can almost shut down completely. Sixth, modesty and tenacity. Individual needles can stay on the tree 40 or 50 years, doing the essential work of photosynthesis without needing to be upgraded to a new model. And the tree itself knows that to survive the wind, to avoid lightning, to protect itself from the weight and hazard of ice storms, it is best to hunker down, stay low, be a bonsai tree. Many bristlecones don't top 30 feet high.

Last, they have a strangely extended lifespan. As one scientist says, they spend the first 2,000 years growing and the next 2,000 years dying, and they are in no hurry to start or stop either side of the equation. This means that even when the main trunk is reduced to bare sculpture, there still can be a single strip of living bark coiling around the trunk from root to final branch. At first glance it looks like a fossil tree, long since passed, and yet a closer look shows a final spray of needles on a final intact branch. They may "go gentle into that good night," in the words of Dylan Thomas, but they do so at a pace that takes centuries to complete.

It is not all wind and rocks in the land of bristlecones. Watch for the big squirrels called marmots, thick-pelted and blunt-nosed. Smaller and much better at begging, chipmunks and golden-mantled squirrels will try to cadge potato chips: Be resolute, since human food is bad for them. Azure mountain bluebirds sally for day-flying moths, while Clark's nutcrackers are black and gray jay relatives that cache seeds and thus inadvertently help plant a new generation of trees.

John Muir called bristlecones "irrepressibly and extravagantly picturesque." It does not take much time spent in the Shulman Grove in order to agree completely.

BADWATER BASIN AND PUPFISH SITES

DEATH VALLEY NATIONAL PARK

Death Valley's unique habitats are revealed by looking for landlocked fish

DIFFICULTY	
Easy	

LENGTH	LOCATION
.5 miles	Badwater Basin is south of Furnace Creek; Salt Creek is north of Beatty Junction; Devils Hole is inside Ash Meadows National Wildlife Refuge

eath Valley and Badwater—do their names say it all? If you want to upsell recreational destinations, these are grim ways to do it. The names Salt Creek and Devils Hole are not much better. Yet these hydrological features have important stories to tell us about geology and evolution, and by seeking out the humble pupfish, we can travel back in time—a time at the end of the Pleistocene when even Death Valley was a greener, wetter, more fish-friendly place.

We start with the lowest place in the United States, the Badwater Basin. This is not one single point but a spring-fed lakebed that consists of miles of salt crust resting on top of gooey, bottomless mud. Everybody wants to take a picture of the sign that points out the elevation, 282 feet below sea level. Equally popular is a "sea level" marker high on a nearby hill.

It does rain at Badwater, and when it does, a visible lake forms, but in the arid climate the water evaporates quickly, returning the landscape to its shimmering white muckiness. Even where the springs seep out most actively, the water is indeed "bad"—too

Badwater is the lowest point in the United States, 282 feet below sea level.

alkaline to be potable, even to mules. The only things that survive in the main pool are algae and snails.

It may seem counterintuitive, then, to recommend Death Valley as a fish-watching site. Bird-watching, maybe, or driving the park's roads on summer nights can be a good way to see snakes and kangaroo rats. Yet the fish are here, and there are two places to seek them out: Salt Creek inside the main park, and Devils Hole, which is managed by Death Valley but located across the state line in Ash Meadows Wildlife Refuge. We visit both sites to learn about the ultimate desert survivors, pupfish.

Devils Hole—no apostrophe—is a 400-foot-deep slit in a cliff whose water is spa-tub warm. The entire world's population of Devils Hole pupfish lives here, mostly in the top 100 feet, with a particular concentration along a single sloping shelf of rock. Tiny little guys, this fish is barely an inch long at its largest. Males are blue, females yellow, and if there is

▲ Devils Hole pupfish are stimulated to breed any time there is an earthquake.

▲ There are two Salt Creek pupfish in this picture, one curled above the other.

an earthquake, everybody flees to deeper water and starts mating. That sounds like the setup for a joke, but it is true. Pupfish eat algae, snails, worms, and park-supplied fish food; the total population in any given spring may be under a few hundred total fish, and so they are both carefully counted and also given a helping hand with supplemental food.

How did they get there is the question, and the answer is many guesses and no obviously correct, single one. They probably have been here since the last great ice sheets melted, which filled the Ash Meadows Basin with water, and as the major lakes dried out, they got left behind. They can live in very salty, low-oxygen water, and with limited winter food, the populations go through "boom and bust" cycles. At the lowest counts, everybody bites their fingernails, hoping a new population will expand next spring.

You can (and should) go to Devils Hole to see them yourself, but be aware that the viewing platform is fenced in, due to overly rowdy human behavior in the past.

Salt Creek in the main part of the park holds an equally unique species, the Salt Creek or Death Valley pupfish. It, too, lives only here, plus a few at a second site called Cottontail Marsh. A half-mile board-walk trail traverses Salt Creek; water flows aboveground beside the trail from November through May. (Fish retreat out of sight to deeper pools when the main streamflow dries up.) Salt Creek is indeed salty, and so the Latin names for the two species make sense, with this kind being *salinas* and the Devils Hole one being *diabolis*. The "pupfish" part comes from mating behavior which supposedly is "puppy-like."

So America's hottest and driest park is home to some of the world's most endangered freshwater fish. And the lowest spot in the Lower 48, Badwater Basin, is only 80 miles as the crow flies from the Lower 48's tallest spot, Mt. Whitney, which is 14,505 feet tall.

Salt Creek in Death Valley is home to an endemic fish, the Salt Creek pupfish. ▾

Due to recent storms, many roads—including Salt Creek's—have been damaged. Be sure to check with Park Service for updated information.

FOSSIL FALLS

A former river that is full of carved, fun-to-explore rocks, plus top-notch lizard-spotting

LOCATION
Off Highway 395 and Cinder Road, north of Little Lake

LENGTH
1 to 2 miles

This site is at its best and at its worst at 10 a.m. on a July morning. Best because that is when the largest lizards are most active on the dark rocks. There are two striking species here, both colorful. The Great Basin or desert collared lizard is orange, green, and blue, with a black-banded neck. They are 10 inches long. Larger and darker and more like an iguana, 16-inch chuckwallas can be seen on the tallest ridges of rock—until you get too close. Then they retreat into narrow crevices, where they gulp in air to expand their bodies, wedging so tightly no kit fox or herpetologist trainee can drag them out. And there are smaller kinds here, too, like the side-blotched lizard, just a few inches long.

‹ A Great Basin collared lizard is ready for its close-up.

And yet July is the worst because of the heat. Unless there are rare midsummer clouds, by ten in the morning it will already be getting too hot to hike. Most people prefer stopping here on a "just right" day in February, when there might be snow on the southern Sierra and when the sun is pleasantly warm, but not an acetylene torch. Of course, in February most lizards are still hibernating, so you will have to make do with ravens and horned larks, rock wrens and loggerhead shrikes.

Chuckwallas are 16 inches long and can puff up with air to wedge themselves firmly into cracks. This is a great place to see them. ▾

The "fossils" here are conceptual, not literal. No T-rex, no fern fronds imprinted in shale. The rock is volcanic, anyway, the one kind of stone that is guaranteed not to contain fossils. Instead, the location name is talking about something that was once roaringly, churningly, abundantly, and stone-carvingly present: an ancient river of

◂ Fossil Falls is
a lava flow that
has been cut and
polished by a
now-extinct river.

◂ Water-sculpted
stones shine in the
sun.

coursing snowmelt, which ran through this canyon at the end of the
last Ice Age. As the melting glaciers filled up Mono Lake and Owens
Lake, there was so much water left over that a prehistoric river ran
down what is now the lower Owens Valley, cutting right through this
basaltic flow. You can see the effect of all that water in the potholes
where pounding water swirled and scoured, and in the smooth rock
lips of once-wide waterfalls. It is a desert now, home to big lizards
and small rain clouds, but if you could have been here 10,000 years
ago, you would not have been able to shout a conversation over the
sound of so much rushing water.

In rare instances, the water comes back; if there are thunder-
storms overhead or upstream, it will be best to wait them out.
Lightning strikes and flash floods are possible.

The other 99.99 percent of the time, you have no restrictions
at this Bureau of Land Management site. The best route to take
is whichever one you want to take, and there are a thousand ways
to enter the canyon and scramble upstream or down. A few shear

drop-offs plunge 40 feet straight down, so be mindful of where you're stepping. That advice also applies because rattlesnakes, though not common, are certainly possible. Look where you step, look where you put your hands, and once in a while look back to memorize the way you have come, to make it easy to pick a straight line to get back to the trailhead.

Other nearby places of interest include Jawbone Canyon, where two giant pipes cross the desert floor. Combined, they contain all the drinking water for the City of Los Angeles. And deeper into the Coso Range, organized tours go to spectacular petroglyphs where hundreds of bighorn sheep and other game animals have been carved into the patina of the rocks. Contact the Maturango Museum for information on access.

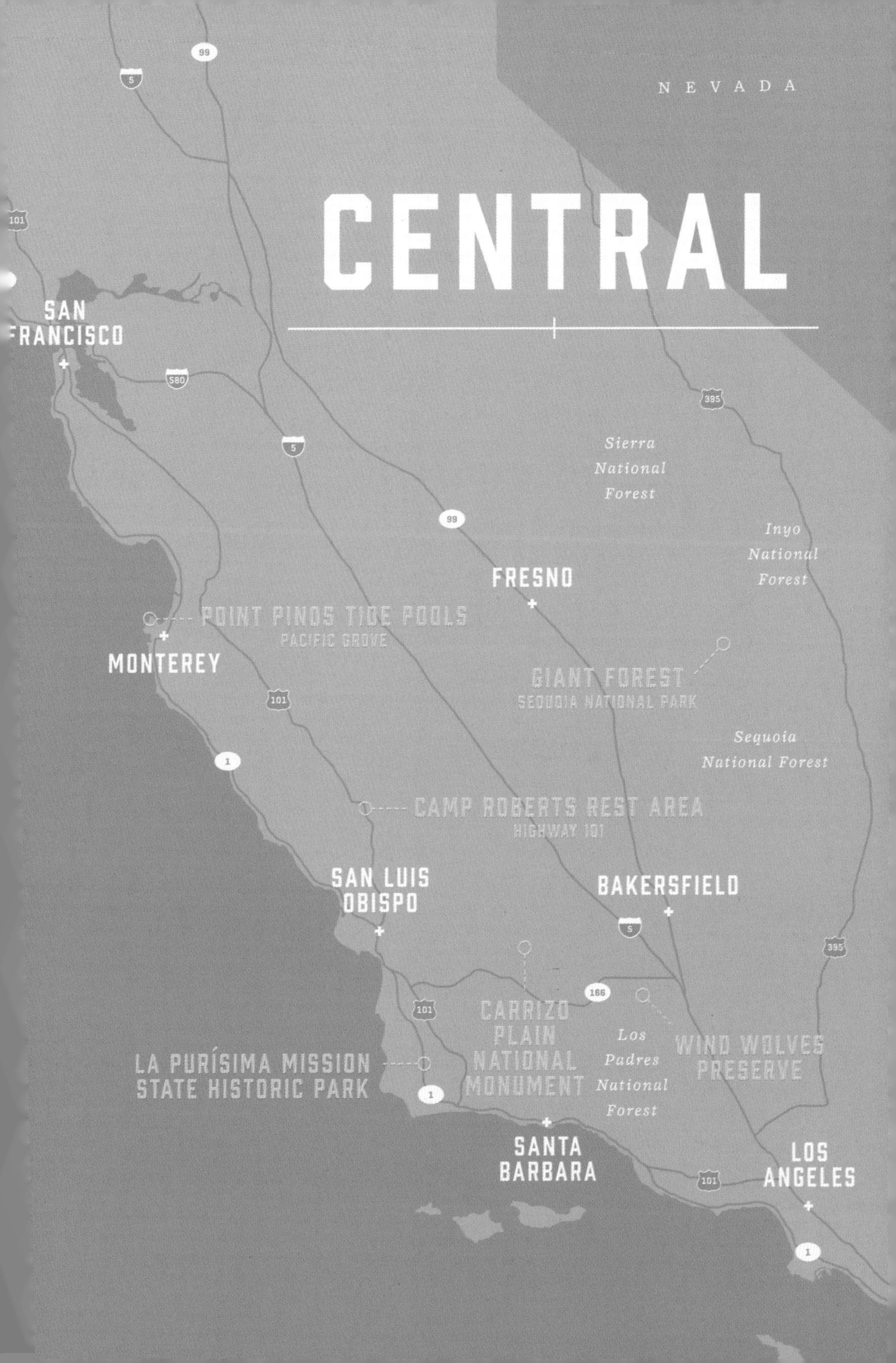

CENTRAL

NEVADA

SAN
FRANCISCO

Sierra
National
Forest

Inyo
National
Forest

FRESNO

POINT PINOS TIDE POOLS
PACIFIC GROVE

MONTEREY

GIANT FOREST
SEQUOIA NATIONAL PARK

Sequoia
National Forest

CAMP ROBERTS REST AREA
HIGHWAY 101

SAN LUIS
OBISPO

BAKERSFIELD

CARRIZO
PLAIN
NATIONAL
MONUMENT

Los
Padres
National
Forest

WIND WOLVES
PRESERVE

LA PURÍSIMA MISSION
STATE HISTORIC PARK

SANTA
BARBARA

LOS
ANGELES

GIANT FOREST

SEQUOIA NATIONAL PARK

Very large, very old, very great trees, plus mule deer and a chance to see a bear

DIFFICULTY
Moderate

LOCATION
Off Wolverton Road, which leaves the Generals Highway just north of the General Sherman Tree

LENGTH
2 miles

The Giant Forest area of Sequoia National Park is, indeed, a forest filled with giants, and each visitor will figure out their own way to explore this inspiring landscape. The word "awesome" has become worn out recently by careless overuse, but if we can remember what it originally meant, which was how something inspired awe, then that word applies here.

I recommend starting with the half-mile walk to the General Sherman Tree and then continuing on the 2-mile loop of the Congress Trail. This will take you past hundreds of monarch sequoias, and—if it's summer, early enough in the day, and you're lucky enough—along the way you might see a deer, bear, coyote, or pileated woodpecker. Also a good choice for wildlife is the Big Trees Trail, a 1-mile loop around a lush meadow.

The term "redwood" gets applied to two different trees in two different habitats. The coastal redwood (page 32) is taller, slimmer, grayer-barked, and (on average) younger. It only lives in the coastal fog belt, Oregon to Santa Cruz. It is still logged commercially.

The redwood of this park is better called sequoia. These trees' bark is always red, and on average they are larger around than coastal redwoods, making a bulkier, more massive tree that can live much longer; giant sequoias can live more than 3,000 years. Many sequoias show a black triangular burn scar at the base where the tree has survived past fires, and in fact usually survived multiple past fires, going back hundreds of years. Thick bark and high branches help protect it, or past tense, *used* to help protect. Recent fires such as the KNP Complex Fire of 2021 have burned so hot and so unstoppably that even the sequoias themselves may not be able to withstand future firestorms.

‹ As the rhyme reminds us, "April showers / bring May flowers." Only, in this case it could be, "Snowmelt's pout / brings the lupines out."

So far as experts can tell, the General Sherman Tree is the world's largest tree, at least if measured by volume. It stands 275 feet tall and is more than 36 feet in diameter at the base. Sixty feet above the base, the Sherman Tree is still 17.5 feet in diameter. Trees this large become difficult for us to comprehend. Estimates put its volume at 52,500 cubic feet of wood, and it's still growing larger each year. How can we visualize that? Not counting the back seat, an average SUV might have 40 cubic feet of cargo storage. If we cut up this tree into firewood, it would take 1,300 SUVs to take away the timber, lined up bumper-to-bumper and stretching over 4 miles. Or to be more organic, the typical mature sequoia tree contains more volume than four and a half blue whales swimming nose-to-tail. (The "half" one will need to be a calf.)

▴ Crow-sized and boldly marked, the pileated woodpecker is one of the most distinctive birds in the Sequoia forest.

When learning trees, some people are tricked, since a smaller species in the same forest has red bark, too. The incense cedar looks red like a sequoia but is much smaller (just "regular tree" sized), and it has flatter, more feathery needles, almost as if the branch has been laid on an ironing board and smoothed out. Sequoia needles are coarser, darker, rounder, and look scalier. Hope chests traditionally used to be made from cedar wood, since it is a strong, non-warping timber that is insect-resistant (at least when

▴ This young buck is still in velvet; later in summer the bare antlers will show.

new), and most people find the odor pleasing. Cedar is so durable that reportedly a house can burn down and cedar chests will survive. Other common trees include white fir, red fir, sugar pine (look for the immense cones), and ponderosa pine.

▴ A bear cub learns the best way to lick ants out of a rotten log.

The bear on the state flag is the grizzly, now extirpated in California, leaving the black bear as our only extant ursine. Sequoia National Park is a good place to see black bears, which as we all know can be other colors besides just black. The usual rules apply: Always give bears a respectful distance, double that distance if cubs are involved, use storage lockers for food and strongly scented items like shampoo, and remember that this is their forest, not yours. We hope we don't need to say it, but when it comes to bears, *no selfies.*

The park does not have elk, so all the deer are exactly that, mule deer. Golden-mantled ground squirrels (page 87) are common in summer, as are Steller's jays (page 68), chipmunks (page 68), and yellow-bellied marmots (page 91).

Giant sequoias occur in a few other areas, as well—the Mariposa Grove in Yosemite National Park is an especially good place to visit— but this park is the best place in the world to see a lot of big trees in one area, and also to have wildlife encounters as part of the same

hike. The Sherman Tree area is also a part of the park that is being very actively managed with controlled burns, making it more secure for the future. You may have seen photographs of the Sherman Tree wrapped in foil blankets as fires in the 2020s drew close; the current management plans hope that this is not ever necessary again.

In my family, my grandparents and great-grandparents have been going to Giant Forest since the close of World War II. With luck, these same trees will be available for my kids' kids' kids to enjoy.

▲ The sequoia tree produces small cones that only open when heated by a forest fire.

POINT PINOS TIDE POOLS

PACIFIC GROVE

Great tide pools, plus sea otters and marine birds

DIFFICULTY
Easy

LENGTH
.25 miles

LOCATION
By Point Pinos Lighthouse, between the Monterey Bay Aquarium and Asilomar Beach

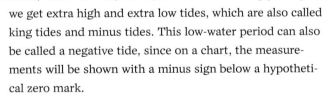

Fishing is not allowed in State Marine Conservation Areas. This abandoned hook and line (just waiting to entangle a sea otter) explains why. ▾

The ocean has high and low tides twice a day, every day of the year. We can blame (or thank) the moon and its gravity for that. The moon tugs water toward itself, and how strongly it does that depends on its angle in relation to us. That bulge in all the water means the ocean stretches out, and it is low tide someplace else. A spinning earth creates centrifugal force, which also contributes to this. Sometimes, when the sun, moon, and earth all line up just right, we get extra high and extra low tides, which are also called king tides and minus tides. This low-water period can also be called a negative tide, since on a chart, the measurements will be shown with a minus sign below a hypothetical zero mark.

Online tide charts can help you discover when high and low tides will be each day, and during winter, when we get the lowest minus tides, that's when you want to grab your water shoes and a windbreaker and head to Pacific Grove. The greatest range of the intertidal zone will be exposed then, making visible things that normally are hidden 7 feet underwater.

There is no assigned route. Park along the road and follow your instincts. One section of coast is no better or

Calm seas and low tides are needed
to access tide pools like these.

worse than another, assuming it is within an hour or two of the low-est tide and assuming rain and wind have not doused your plans with storm surge and salt spray. Watch the open sea, though, wherever you are, in case a sneaker wave races in, and also to be able to spot sea otters, harbor seals, California sea lions, and even the occasional pod of inshore bottlenose dolphins. Whales can sometimes be seen from shore, but it's more reliable (and more fun) to go out on a dedicated whale-watching boat.

For the tide pools themselves, here is a mini-bestiary to guide you in your investigations.

Sea Anemones. These are sit-and-wait predators, using tenta-cles to sting fish and any lesser items that cross within reach. If a falling tide strands them in the open air, they clench up into a pebble-dotted green fist that is a bit squishy to the touch. But when the tide returns, sea anemones blossom again into medusa flowers, with waving, mobile tentacles always ready to direct things into the green ovals of their mouths.

The sea anemone has stinging tenta-cles to catch small fish. ⏷

Sponges. Some people mistake this group for corals. Brightest and easiest to spot are the orange mats of red sponge, genus *Microciona*. Sponges do not have mouths but suck seawater in through small pores, which they filter for edible particles and squirt out.

Mussels. Blue-black and 2–8 inches long, the California mussel forms dense colonies called beds. Pound on, harsh waves. Mussels are so stoutly built and firmly anchored they can endure the fiercest Pacific storms. It is a two-shell mollusk, and when exposed to air, it "clams up," shutting the two halves so tightly together it seems they are joined with epoxy. Sea stars and/or curious children may try to pry them open. Both are usually unsuccessful.

Snails. Black turban snails are an inch long and have a shell that fits the name. Brown turbans are taller, paler, and favor deeper water. Periwinkles are purple, brown, or black and they graze algae; their shell looks like a regular garden snail's, but drawn into more of a teardrop profile.

Limpets. A tiny domed shell defines a limpet, sort of like the profile of the island of Hawai'i, if Hawai'i were scaled down to thumbnail size. Keyhole limpets expel water out of the small "keyhole" opening at the top their shells. Ribbed limpets have corrugations in their shells like the ridges on ruffled potato chips. Owl limpets can be 4 inches across and bulldoze back and forth across their small garden plot of rock, grazing on algae and trying to bully away any other potential nibblers and settlers.

Barnacles. A barnacle starts life as swimming larvae, but eventually settles down, cementing itself to a rock and building a volcano-shaped house. Its glue is so strong that the shell remains attached to the rock even after the main occupant has died. Acorn barnacles are small and not particular: They need to be washed over by seawater so they can filter feed, but whether that is on the Monterey shore or while attached to the hull of a yacht, that is all the same to them. The gooseneck barnacle is longer and more colonial, and can look like (and be found with) California mussels. Fun fact: Irish novelist James Joyce's wife was named Nora Barnacle.

Crabs. So many crabs, including lined, kelp, rock, purple shore, and green shore. Don't worry about the names and just watch them scuttle and scurry, waving fierce claws to keep you at bay. Hermit crabs also live here, one of many reasons not to take home seashells.

Sea Stars. Technically one is not supposed to call them "starfish" (since they're not fish), even though everybody (including this author) still does. The largest ones, usually red or purple, are the ochre sea stars, with five arms and a pebbly, knobby surface. They are predators, hoping to find a mussel, pry it open, and slurp it out. Bat stars, usually smaller, have their five legs more joined, less distinct. They can be red but also blotchy white and orange, purple, blue, or green. Sunflower stars can grow to be the largest starfish in the world and have even more arms—up to twenty or even twenty-four.

▲ Bat stars are small, usually bright, sea stars.

Sea Urchins. Purple pincushions, they graze algae, scavenge detritus, or chew divots out of kelp. Sea otters eat them and gulls will try, as well as large fish and the largest sea stars. One can't blame urchins for wanting to be hidden under their porcupine coats.

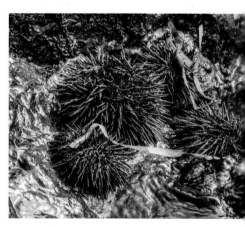

▲ As the tide falls, a cluster of sea urchins emerges into view.

Birds. Just a few, in particular, to note. Everybody knows gulls, and Monterey has ten species in winter. Those can have up to eight plumage cycles each, and then gulls hybridize across species lines creating head-scratching half-and-halfs; so the bottom line is that seagulls only exist to make field guide authors rich. The best answer is just to say no and not even get started with gull identification, which is a contentious and deeply unsatisfying hobby. Easier to appreciate are

⁂ An adult western gull surveys its tidal domain.

the black oystercatchers. As crab-grabbers and mollusk-crackers, they, too, relish low tide, and with a reasonable size (about like a small duck), pink legs, black bodies, yellow eyes, and coral-red bills, they brighten any shoreline afternoon.

And some history . . . Monterey's most famous tide pooler was Ed Ricketts, fictionalized as Doc in John Steinbeck's *Cannery Row*. Ricketts is also the scientific and philosophical center of Steinbeck's *The Log from the Sea of Cortez*, a classic both of marine biology and travel narrative. Ricketts was a biologist whose handbook to intertidal life has remained in print for 50 years. He died in a car accident and there are several monuments to him around town. Here is one Ricketts quote that deserves to be remembered: "Children must be very wise and secret to tolerate adults at all."

A visit to Point Pinos is about changing scale and expectation. As you squat down to figure out what's going on in the bottom of a pool of trapped water, your circle of attention may zoom down to be just a few inches wide. Going slowly makes sense here. Not only is moss slick and a boulder covered in barnacles painfully sharp to tumble into, but studying the "in between" parts of the ocean offers the best chance to see the sudden flash of an octopus or the red flare of a hidden crab. If your camera has a macro setting, use that, too.

"In an age of speed, I began to think nothing could be more exhilarating than going slow"—so writes travel expert Pico Iyer. He adds, "In an age of distraction, nothing can feel more luxurious than paying attention. And in an age of constant movement, nothing is more urgent than sitting still."

CAMP ROBERTS REST AREA
HIGHWAY 101

California's roadside rests have nature, too, including this one that is a good stop for the endemic yellow-billed magpie

DIFFICULTY
Easy

LOCATION
The southbound 101 Camp Roberts Rest Area is south of Bradley, north of Nacimiento, and fifteen minutes from Paso Robles

LENGTH
.25 miles

California's roadside rests (also called rest areas, rest stops, and wayside rests) offer interstate travelers a chance to stretch, go to the bathroom, walk the dog, and even bird-watch. Some locations are more productive than others. One favorite site is the southbound 101 rest stop near Camp Roberts, which in the past has been a good place to try for yellow-billed magpie, a California endemic related to jays and crows. Its yellow beak and iridescent tail make it stand out from any other bird on the highway. One guidebook calls it "boisterous" and describes it as "a riot of black, white, shimmering blue-green, and yellow." This species normally likes oak groves and riparian forests, but at least here on the 101, it also likes to hop around the picnic tables, hunting for tortilla chip shards and lost sandwich crusts.

There are 87 roadside rests in California, and you can make two firm predictions about them. The first is that ten percent will be closed on any given day, since the managing agency, Caltrans, is retrofitting them all to be more ADA-accessible and to use water more wisely. As we go to press, Camp Roberts Rest Area has just reopened after being closed for a year and a half. And do note, the southbound side is usually birdier than the northbound.

▲ The yellow-billed magpie is endemic to California.

▲ A Botta's pocket gopher makes a brief above-ground appearance.

The other prediction one can make with certainty is that each area has more nature than the average visitor notices. At the southbound Camp Roberts site, the online birding reference eBird lists 86 species, from hawks to herons to an out-of-range East Coast sparrow. The most glorious of these is the yellow-billed magpie, but California thrashers and Nuttall's woodpeckers would be good finds on any oak woodland hike. They are both frequently seen here, along with dark-eyed juncos, yellow-rumped warblers, titmice, and jays. One has simply to stop and look.

Larger animals can be spotted as well. At the Camp Roberts southbound site, tule elk can sometimes be seen just on the other side of the fence, and most California roadside rests offer a chance to see Botta's pocket gopher. It creates the dirt mounds in lawns and bare earth; the "pockets" are cheek pouches for storing food. Where there are gophers, it makes sense there will be gopher snakes, and the photograph at the top of page 118 was taken on the southbound I–5, at the Westley Rest Area, where the 580 comes in from East Bay. Middle of the day and the area was busy as can be, and yet almost nobody noticed a 3-foot snake patrolling the grounds. It found what it wanted (a fresh burrow), and down it went.

The same stop had nesting ravens, a passing Swainson's hawk, and two species of blackbird. Just down the road, an active colony of cliff swallows was nesting under a highway overpass.

In California, the idea of roadside shade trees became popular before (but was extended by) the Bureau of Highways, established in 1895. Plans have always been ambitious; to be well-rested is to be safe, and rest means trees and nature. Through the 1930s, many roadside fountains, picnic areas, and scenic overviews were built by Depression-era work crews. Each lasted until it didn't, since post-war road-widening and road-straightening often meant former pullouts and lay-bys had to be paved over.

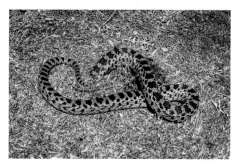

▲ This gopher snake is about to disappear down a gopher hole.

By the 1960s, there was a new master plan ready, with a grand vision to replace previous sites with a statewide network of 257 rest areas. Lovely idea, but it was missing one essential component: funding. No money means no new rest stops. That leaves Caltrans where it is today, trying to make do with what it has. On holiday weekends on I–5, the only thing longer than the wait to park is the line to the women's restroom.

Yet birds are there no matter what. In the desert, they may be ravens and western kingbirds, while near agricultural areas it might be mostly crows and Brewer's

▲ An out-of-range white-throated sparrow seems perfectly at home at the Camp Roberts Rest Area on Highway 101.

blackbirds. Some of my best pictures of golden-crowned sparrows were taken at rest areas. In the Eastern Sierra, one fall there was an eastern warbler called an ovenbird at the Coso Junction rest stop, and according to my notes, "At 06:12 it was feeding on cockroaches under the lights of the north office building." Donner Summit on I–80 has chickadees, red crossbills, sapsuckers, and pine siskins. The reports on the website iNaturalist for the westbound side of Donner Summit include multiple species of dragonflies, wolf lichen, jelly spot fungus, Sierra tiger lily, and one September evening, a black bear "checking the trash cans in the middle of the night."

CARRIZO PLAIN NATIONAL MONUMENT

A wide-open grassland with kit foxes, badgers, and spring wildflowers

DIFFICULTY
Easy

LENGTH
.25 to 4.5 miles

LOCATION
Soda Lake Road, between Highways 166 and 58

Badgers are low-bodied, stripe-faced diggers, common here but not often seen. ▾

First things first: this is a big place. At 246,812 acres, and at 50 miles long and 15 miles wide, Carrizo is comprised of former and current ranches now set aside as open space, and it remains the largest native grassland in California. What one does and where one goes on the Carrizo Plains—usually said as plural, despite the official name—depends on goals, time of year, and how deeply we are or are not in a drought when you visit.

If it's a superbloom year, there will be flowers, which is a statement better typed like this: THERE WILL BE FLOWERS.

Expect poppies, of course, and also goldfields, fiddlenecks, tidy tips, purple owl's clover, desert candle, mustard, and phacelia—nature's full florist shop will be open for business. There could even be some light traffic, unusual for such a rarely visited park.

Or if it's a wet winter, otherwise dry Soda Lake may be full, and could even have white pelicans and sandhill cranes, plus ducks, shorebirds, and short-eared owls. Take the boardwalk trail in that case and bring a spotting scope if you can borrow one.

But then—

And here comes the disclaimer at the bottom of the contract. If it's a dry year and it's summer and it's the middle of the day, you could end up wondering, "What's all the fuss about?" In that case, just wait until after dark. Mammal-watchers know a secret. (And yes, just as there are train-spotters and bird-watchers, there are people who go out to see mammals—and not just tigers, but the small obscure stuff, like pack rats and pallid bats.) After dark is when your car headlights or a handheld flashlight may pick up the eyeshine of a kit fox or a badger, and when the park's main road comes alive with the hopping, scurrying shapes of kangaroo rats, deer mice, pocket mice, desert cottontails, and black-tailed jackrabbits.

Two species, in particular, attract hard-core mammal-spotters: Heermann's kangaroo rat and the giant kangaroo rat. Don't take "giant" too literally . . . it's still a modest-sized rodent, all in all, and definitely not a capybara or some kind of feral possum-beaver. However, it is the largest "k-rat" in North America and so is interesting that way; it's interesting, too, to the coyotes and foxes that want

Carrizo is wide views and no towns, and, after dark, a busy community of animals.

to eat it. Adolphus Lewis Heermann is remembered in the bird field guides for a "reverse" gull, the Heermann's gull, which is white-headed and gray-bodied, the opposite of most other seagulls. His kangaroo rat is tan with a long tail and a bounding leap, and like other kangaroo rats, harvests seeds and lives underground in a network of tunnels.

Other inhabitants of the nightscape include skunks, coyotes, tarantulas, barn owls, and great horned owls.

The small daytime squirrels with white tails curled over their backs are Nelson's or San Joaquin antelope squirrels. They eat seeds, plants, and insects, and while they gladly will drink water, they do not need it to survive, or at least not to survive for many months on end.

Speaking of antelope, pronghorn live at Carrizo, thanks to reintroductions in the 1980s, and are most often noticed on the

▸ This kangaroo rat at a Carrizo campground is not sure whether to run away or beg for sunflower seeds.

Highway 58–Soda Lake end of the basin. Often called pronghorn antelope, they were once common through the Central Valley and along the coastal plains, and their former presence is remembered in place names like "Antelope Valley" (of which California has many). The pronghorn is not an antelope, despite the name, nor is it a deer. It is just itself, no more, no less, with distant connections to the giraffe and the okapi.

The pronghorn is the fastest land animal in the Western Hemisphere, designed to outrun a now-extinct species of cheetah. All that speed and yet it could not outrun the twentieth century:

⁎ Spring in Carrizo Plain Monument means flowers—sometimes more, sometimes fewer, but always something.

⁎ Pronghorn are often called "antelope," but they are more closely related to giraffes.

Pronghorn herds disappeared in California due to fences, hunting, changing grass regimes, and falling water tables. While not thriving at Carrizo, the reintroduced pronghorn have not completely died out, either; if you see any, count yourself among that day's most blessed visitors.

Hiking trails to consider include the 1-mile San Andreas Fault hike along Wallace Creek, the previously mentioned boardwalk at Soda Lake, and the Painted Rock Trail, which starts 2 miles south of the Goodwin Education Center.

No matter when you come, start with a full gas tank, since there are no services, and be ready for dust, since most of the park is traversed by a wide, graded, but often corrugated dirt road. The only time the main road is not dusty is after it rains, when, of course, it will be muddy—very muddy. Don't let that stop you; it is worth making the journey just to have an idea of what California used to look like, and, if civilization manages to snuff itself out, what it will look like once more.

WIND WOLVES PRESERVE

Five ecologies converge at an under-visited park with tule elk and a chance for coyote or bobcat, or maybe even a puma

DIFFICULTY
Moderate

LOCATION
Off Highway 166, 10 miles west from I–5

LENGTH
5 miles

A fall stand of cottonwoods blazes gold along San Emigdio Canyon Trail.

F ive ecologies converge at Wind Wolves Preserve. These include grassland, the Mojave Desert, and the junction of three mountain ranges—the Transverse Range, the Coast Range, and the southern edge of the Sierra Nevada. The preserve spans a mile of vertical relief, going from 600 feet to more than 6,000. If you were to hike from entrance to summit, the plant mix would reveal microclimate and elevation as clearly as a topo map. The valley floor starts out with cactus and saltbush in the scrubby grasslands, then transitions into oak savanna with cottonwood wetlands higher up. As the oak forest ascends, the tree mix starts to include more juniper and pinyon. At the preserve's highest elevations, the forest changes again, becoming pure stands of ponderosa pine and big-cone spruce.

Through all the elevation layers, mountain lions hunt mule deer and tule elk, though those prey items are easier to see than the puma itself. Coyotes and bobcats are also possible, especially in winter, and kit foxes den near the entrance road. With all wildlife-centered trips, being up and out early is best, especially in summer, and midweek usually is better than weekends.

Our recommended hike at this preserve, managed by the Wildlands Conservancy, goes up San Emigdio Canyon, pauses at a picnic site, and comes back downcanyon the same way it went up. If you're on mountain bikes, a parallel choice uses service roads instead, though that route has to forfeit hiking by (and resting under) the willows and cottonwoods of the riparian forest. You will probably cover more ground but hear and see fewer birds. On either route, keep looking up: Condors are always possible.

Is there nature when we can't see it and only know about it conceptually? On this hike you may see elk tracks or fox tracks; you may find a roosting owl or hear (and see) a coyote.

A winter coyote pauses its hunt to study the photographer. ▾

What about the rest of the natural order, things too small or shy to interact with? There is a tiny little guy, the Buena Vista Lake shrew (*Sorex ornatus relictus*), related to a parent species, the ornate shrew. Shrews are black-furred, pointy-nosed, and mouse-sized. Shrew facts include the reality that their metabolism races along at such full throttle that they need to eat the equivalent of their own body weight every day. If you're a hefty guy, as I am, that would be 900 Quarter Pounders a day. Some shrews are venomous, some shrews can echolocate, and all shrews have hearts that beat a thousand times a minute. (Elephant heart rates are more typically 30 beats per minute—*boom, boom, boom,* a slow and steady drum.)

◂ The chocolate lily is a California endemic that can be seen here in spring. Another name is "mission bells."

◂ Poppies and new grass create a soothing vista at Wind Wolves Preserve.

Shrews weigh only a few grams—about the same as six paper clips—yet they eat anything and everything, including ants, spiders, slugs, crickets, earthworms, mice, and even baby rats. Small but mighty—and also small but rarely seen. Because of habitat loss in the San Joaquin Valley, the Buena Vista Lake shrews are probably the most endangered mammals in the United States. When you hike here, you probably won't see a shrew, but isn't it cool to know they are so close by? Just under some wet brush by a stream, *right there,* that could be the den of one now.

The preserve name puzzles some visitors. The "wind wolves" moniker references grasses blowing in the wind, not aeolian canids. There was a real wolf here recently, though. In 2021, the young male wolf known as OR-93 wandered south through almost all of California, from Modoc County past Yosemite, over to Monterey, and south through Wind Wolves Preserve, before being killed by a car on I–5 near Lebec. He was the first wolf verified to have been in Southern California in 99 years.

While wolves have their haters, the actual truth is that wolf packs pose little threat to life or property. This book says, "Bring back the wolves!" And in fact, while we're at it, having now successfully saved the condors, let's bring back the grizzly bears, too.

LA PURÍSIMA MISSION STATE HISTORIC PARK

An easy chaparral hike along a historic waterworks

DIFFICULTY
Easy

LOCATION
Purísima Road, 3 miles northeast of central Lompoc

LENGTH
1 to 2 miles

Welcome to the second and final Misión La Purísima Concepción de María Santísima, relocated here in 1813 after an earlier version in downtown Lompoc was destroyed in an earthquake. Missions in California are being reappraised, and the previous narratives have become richer and more complete as we consider the perspectives of the Native Americans that the missions displaced, converted, and in some cases enslaved. To be simply factual, these things are sequentially true: The Chumash lived here for thousands of years; in the late eighteenth century, Spain began building missions in Alta California; in time, these churches were taken over by a newly independent Mexico, and, not long after, almost all were abandoned. Most missions we see today, including La Purísima, are twentieth-century reconstructions. The buildings and associated landscape of La Purísima are managed by the state park system as a historical site, and this mission (unlike most others today) is no longer an official part of the Catholic church.

A good route for a walk is up the Las Zanjas Trail past the old well house, and then do a loop around the low valley back

After the first church collapsed, the new adobe walls were made thicker than usual, to withstand stronger earthquakes. ▾

◄ Mission-style architecture like this still influences building design today.

to the mission grounds proper. Expect company; locals know to come here for easy access to open space. Multiple trails interconnect and you can pick a route based on shade, birdsong, and your energy levels.

To hike here does mean thinking about history and our relationship to it. When the current mission was built, with its oak beams and thick, pink-washed adobe walls, each Spanish mission was like medieval village. It had to be self-contained, from tanneries and blacksmith shops to gardens for medicinal herbs. On-site kilns fired rooftiles, orchards supplied fruit, and there had to be inventive infrastructure. La Purísima, for example, had an intricate 3-mile water system that included an aqueduct and underground piping. Tallow for candles and hides for leather were export goods, and that meant eventually 20,000 cattle and sheep grazed the local hills, along with hundreds of horses, mules, and oxen.

Now things are quieter, calmer, and on the main hike, more natural, since you can appreciate the soaring red-tailed hawks and the flowering coffeeberry bushes which have returned to re-wild and repopulate the once-overgrazed chaparral. California sycamores line the creek, and California thrashers hop and scratch in leaf duff using their long, scythe-like bills. Towhees often join them, plain brown as well, but towhees have sparrow-like seed-crusher bills, not the curved hook of a thrasher. Nuttall's woodpeckers reveal themselves with their *pita-pita-pita* call rattled off in rapid succession. Painted

lady butterflies join skippers and hairstreaks in seeking out sunlit blossoms, while scrub jays *"shrenk shrenk"* at each other, arguing over acorns.

The abundant and frantic ground squirrels on the parade ground and along the meadow edges are all the same species, California ground squirrel, which some field guides call the Beechey ground squirrel, after its Latin name. (Frederick Beechey was a British mapmaker and sea captain.) They graze on plants, harvest seeds, and scrounge successfully after picnic scraps. When a busload of school-children arrives, do all the ground squirrels chirp with glee? Probably yes, and the jays pass the word, too.

A final note here on the buildings. Most date from the 1930s and '40s (with the most recent one added in 1983), but we know from contemporary sketches and reports, and then from late-nineteenth-century photographs and paintings, that the CCC work crews got it right. They used the extant ruins and historically appropriate methods to rebuild the site accurately. (They did add some judicious and well-concealed concrete and rebar along the way.)

This visual vocabulary of Mission-style and Mission Revival architecture lives on today. In visiting La Purísima, you are experiencing the granddaddy template that gave us the Fort Winfield Scott barracks at the Presidio in San Francisco, Union Station in downtown Los Angeles, the Animal Science building at UC Davis, all the tile-roofed subdivisions in the vast and uniform California suburbs, and every Taco Bell at every exit along Interstate 5.

◂ A wren-tit explores the herb garden's rosemary. It weaves a cup-shaped nest out of sage bark and spiderwebs.

◂ Painted lady butterflies wait until the sun comes out to fly; when it is cold and wet, you won't see them.

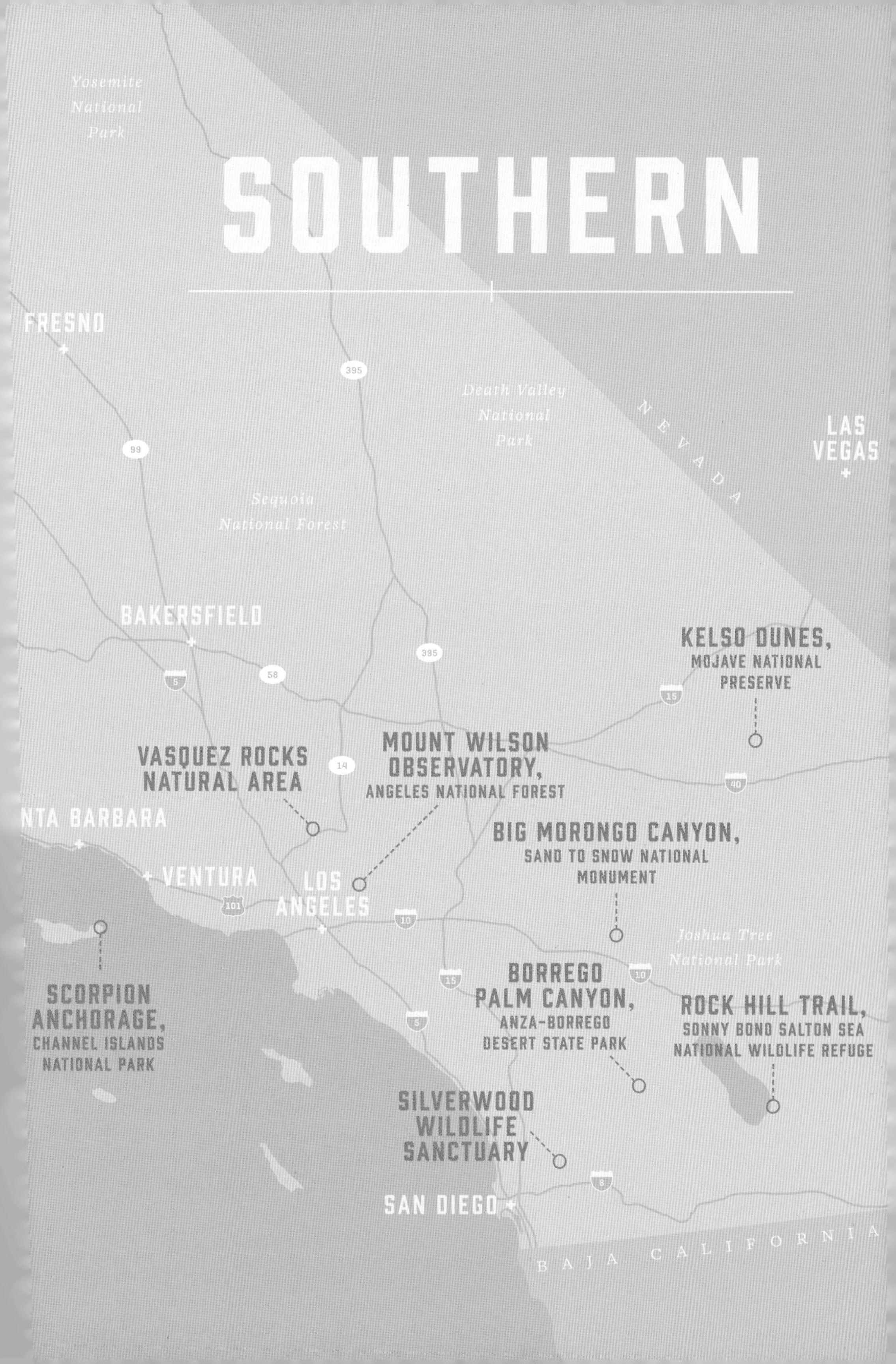

SOUTHERN

Yosemite National Park

FRESNO

395

Death Valley National Park

NEVADA

LAS VEGAS

99

Sequoia National Forest

BAKERSFIELD

395

KELSO DUNES, MOJAVE NATIONAL PRESERVE

5

58

15

40

VASQUEZ ROCKS NATURAL AREA

14

MOUNT WILSON OBSERVATORY, ANGELES NATIONAL FOREST

NTA BARBARA

BIG MORONGO CANYON, SAND TO SNOW NATIONAL MONUMENT

VENTURA

LOS ANGELES

101

10

Joshua Tree National Park

SCORPION ANCHORAGE, CHANNEL ISLANDS NATIONAL PARK

15

10

BORREGO PALM CANYON, ANZA-BORREGO DESERT STATE PARK

ROCK HILL TRAIL, SONNY BONO SALTON SEA NATIONAL WILDLIFE REFUGE

5

SILVERWOOD WILDLIFE SANCTUARY

8

SAN DIEGO

BAJA CALIFORNIA

SCORPION ANCHORAGE

CHANNEL ISLANDS NATIONAL PARK

Sorry for the exclamation points, but very! cute! foxes! (and an endemic jay, plus lots of dolphins)

DIFFICULTY
Medium to Hard

LOCATION
East end of Santa Cruz Island, usually reached by boat from Ventura Harbor

LENGTH
4.5 miles (the longest option)

We all know that everything in nature has equal value, from the squinched-up faces of roosting bats to the glossy black dung beetles called stink bugs. And yet, even knowing that and believing it fully, it's still hard not to say that some things, like puppy dogs and baby pandas, are just so dang *cute*, and certainly cuter than, say, a turkey vulture or a road-killed toad.

The one animal into which the Powers-That-Be poured all their leftover cuteness was the island fox, *Urocyon littoralis*. It once was a regular mainland gray fox, but either through "rafting" (coming over the water on floating vegetation) or via deliberate release by the Chumash, it arrived in the Channel Islands 6,000 years ago and evolved to be smaller—much smaller. Adults usually only weigh 4 or 5 pounds, and they're a foot and a half long, not counting the tail—which is to say this is a fox that is the size of a house cat and perhaps lighter, depending how much extra food Mittens has been sneaking between meals.

Island foxes can climb trees just like the mainland form, and what they eat varies by island. On Santa Rosa Island, the preferred foods are deer mice, Jerusalem crickets, beetles, and earwigs. On other Channel Islands, diet includes the fruit from cactus, manzanita, saltbushes, and sea figs, as well as insects and mice. Occasionally, foxes forage along the shoreline for crabs and other marine life. And on Santa Cruz, especially around Scorpion Anchorage, they are extremely adroit at opening backpacks and raiding camp food. Between the foxes and the ravens, you may feel like you need to wrap your ice chest in a Kevlar vest and add two or three motion-sensor detectors.

These foxes almost didn't make it. In the 1990s, native bald eagles had been in decline for twenty years and were slowly being replaced by not-native-here golden eagles. Bald eagles eat fish, while golden eagles eat cat-sized animals like foxes; the foxes were getting wiped out. The National Park Service and its partners captive-bred replacement foxes while capturing the golden eagles and replacing them with bald eagles (which are large enough to keep the goldens

◦ An island fox perks up—"Is that an unattended backpack over there?"

away). The plan worked and everything is back as it was, pre-decline. Of course, each cog of the machine interacts with every other cog. With the foxes back, the even-smaller-than-foxes island spotted skunks, which had been increasing—or at least were increasingly being seen around the campground—withdrew back into the denser, less accessible canyons. The two species can and do coexist, but the foxes are the dominant island land mammal (after humans).

All visitors get to Santa Cruz Island by boat—either your own or with a commercial service like Island Packers. Watch for dolphins

The rugged and beautiful Santa Cruz Island, home to foxes and much more. ▾

on the crossing, and for pink-footed, sooty, and black-vented shear-waters. And sometimes, if your luck is running high and it is spring or summer, there could even be humpback, fin, or blue whales.

You will be met by a ranger at the dock and given the usual safety tips, including strong admonitions not to feed the foxes.

If you want to just snorkel or hang out at the beach, no need to go any further inland than the arrival dock. Foxes might be there or a half-mile away around the campground. To see the endemic island scrub jays, think about doing the Scorpion Canyon Loop Trail.

‹ Kelp forests create artistic patterns in the water.

This 1950s minesweeper in Scorpion Harbor intrigues divers. How did it sink? Nobody is sure. ›

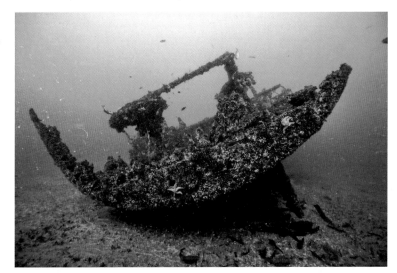

You'll need water, sunscreen, and probably a sack lunch. The park service says this: "To avoid a steep climb, hike clockwise starting on the Smugglers Road toward the oil well and eventually down into Scorpion Canyon and back out to the beach. Hike off-trail into the right (or northwest) fork of Scorpion Canyon to see the island scrub-jay, but be prepared for extremely rocky conditions."

Two miles round-trip from the beach is the Cavern Point Loop, another good choice even though it doesn't have jays. Again, I concur with the National Park Service: "Magnificent coastal vistas and seasonal whale viewing. To avoid a steep climb, hike clockwise, beginning from campground (near site #22) and looping back to Scorpion Anchorage. From Cavern Point, you may also follow the North Bluff Trail west for 2 miles out to Potato Harbor."

If you come over on the commercial boat service, your round-trip ticket will include a required departure time, a bit like catching the last bus out of Dodge. Sunburned and laughing, most people seem sad to go. Camping is also possible, with reservations needed most weekends.

VASQUEZ ROCKS NATURAL AREA

Fun sci-fi rocks and desert chaparral plants are found at a famous filming location

DIFFICULTY
Easy

LOCATION
By Agua Dulce and Escondido Canyon Roads, off the 14 Freeway

LENGTH
.5 to 2 miles

You've been here before, even if you have never been here before. Vasquez Rocks park, an hour from Los Angeles, has been the backdrop for everything from the original *Star Trek* television series to the live-action *Flintstones* movie. Over the years, hundreds of Westerns were filmed here, as were hundreds more student films and fashion shoots. These rocks deserve their own star on Hollywood Boulevard.

The rocks started as layers of sand and mud in delta fans under the sea, plus a scattering of harder stones mixed in by flash floods. Meanwhile, the earth's crust was moving, shifting, and rearranging; nothing was static and everything, even wide expanses of seabed, eventually would be shifted someplace new. That was accelerated 25 million years ago when the North American Plate began to push against the Pacific Plate. Their slow-motion collision caused the previously flat layers to buckle and rise. Compression had already turned the deposited sand into sandstone, and uplifting tilted these layers so they pointed up at an angle, like dinner plates drying in a dish rack. If we had a long enough roll of film, playing it back would reveal an amazing sequence of crushing, squeezing, folding, and lifting.

To explore Vasquez, after checking out the visitor center, take the short dirt road east to where it ends in a large, informal parking area. You will see rocks on three sides: pick a slab and start climbing. This is stone that was never glacier polished, and since the average rainfall is low, rocks don't get worn smooth by water. That

Uptilted sandstone slabs invite endless scrambling. ▸

means the rough grit of the sandstone offers firm grip to most hands and sneakers. It is not a piton and Perlon rope park, but a "Hey Mom, look at me!" park.

Plants here reveal a mix of desert and chaparral communities. Yuccas thrust up tall flower stalks, or maybe on your visit the hollyleaf cherries will be ripe. (Birds like them more than people do.) The black bird with red eyes and white wing flashes is the phainopepla. Most

⌃ Hollyleaf cherry is a plant
whose name is exactly correct.

◂ The visitor center's design
quotes the adjacent rocks.

trees are California juniper. Western fence lizards do push-ups to flash
blue bellies and warn off rivals. Cobblestone lichens and crater lichens
add color and texture to the shady sides of boulders. Years ago, an
Eagle Scout project added large wooden signs to the trails, helping to
identify the plants. Not all of the signs are still accurate: plants die,
soil erodes, fires burn and cleanse. Half are right and half are not. It
turns out that well-made signs can live longer than the vegetation can.

The site name remembers Tiburcio Vásquez, a romanticized bandito from the 1870s who may not have been quite such a courtly Robin Hood as stories want to pretend. He did hide out here, and in nearby Littlerock and Lake Elizabeth, though he was captured near the La Brea Tar Pits, then tried and hanged in San Francisco. Until capture, he and his gang had moved freely up and down the state. Modern-day trans-state travelers include Pacific Crest Trail thru-hikers, some of whom you may see, since the Pacific Crest Trail passes through Vasquez Rocks on its long journey from Mexico to Canada.

◄ California buckwheat looks like a plant topped with cotton balls . . .

▲ . . . but up close, each buckwheat "ball" turns out to be a cluster of smaller flowers.

MOUNT WILSON OBSERVATORY

ANGELES NATIONAL FOREST

DIFFICULTY
Easy

*Mile-high pines and an observatory where
the age of the universe was discovered*

LENGTH
.5 to 2 miles

LOCATION
Off of Angeles Crest Highway, at the end
of Mt. Wilson Red Box Road

nce upon a time, the only thing in the sky were the stars, plus a few stray planets and the oddball comet or two. Then, in 1919, along came Edwin Hubble, and everything changed. Using the 100-inch Hooker Telescope on Mount Wilson, Hubble's discovery that countless galaxies exist beyond our own Milky Way galaxy revolutionized our understanding of the universe. What looked like single points of light were in fact far-off aggregates of many, many millions of stars, and more than that, they were all rushing away from us—and so the expansion of the universe was first documented here. After many nights of careful measurements, Hubble estimated the expansion rate of the universe to be 500 kilometers per second per megaparsec, or what is now a unit of measure known as the Hubble Constant.

No wonder NASA named a space telescope after him.

You can see Hubble's 100-inch Hooker Telescope today if you visit the Mount Wilson Observatory. This mountain range represents a more familiar silhouette than some people guess just from the name. If you ever have watched

World-class astronomy happens underneath this humble dome. ▾

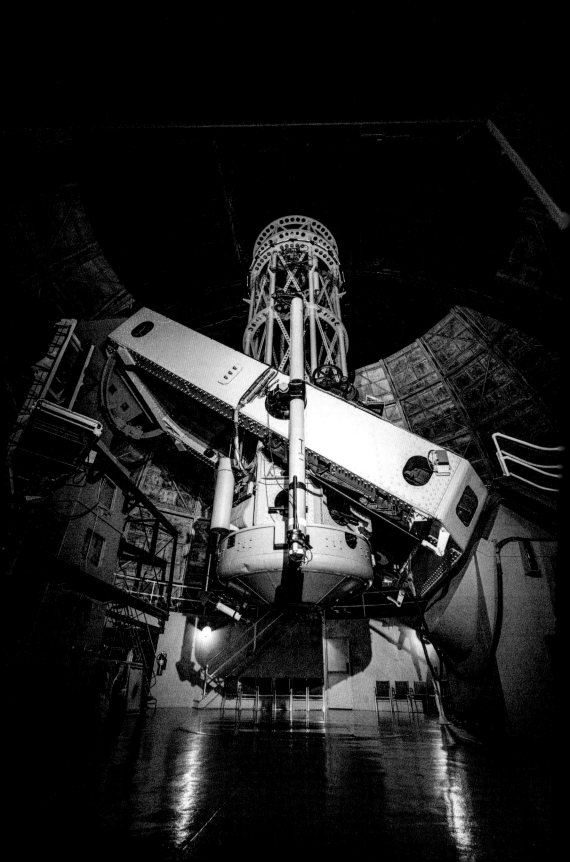

⊳ Views from the trail include Los Angeles in one direction and the rest of the San Gabriel Range in the other.

⊳ When it was built, the 100-inch Hooker Telescope was the largest in the world.

a Tournament of Roses Parade, you have almost certainly seen the snowy mountains across which the cameras pan in the background. That means you have seen Mt. Wilson, too, since it is a slightly taller bump in the long, jagged ridgeline of the San Gabriel Mountains' west-facing slopes. There are other telescopes here, and a cluster of current and former radio and television antennae serving the broadcast needs of a pre-cable, pre–satellite dish, pre-internet Los Angeles.

This entire summit ridge is scenic, historic, economically valuable, and scientifically essential. Every time there is a big fire, crews work hard to save the domes and the telescopes. Fires have burned up to, around, across, and through Mount Wilson, but so far (touch wood) the science infrastructure has escaped destruction.

Fit and ambitious hikers can reach Mt. Wilson from the Pasadena lowlands, but the car route means driving into the center of the range behind it and taking a spur road back west. Park at the end of the road and follow the signs to the observatory complex.

The view from the summit trails varies from smoggy to foggy to "Hey, I can see the ocean!" (Smoggy is most common, alas.) Trails connect the buildings and vistas, or radiate away (Rim Trail, Echo

Rock Trail), allowing you to mix and match routes and fill the day with as much walking as you have mood for.

    Western gray squirrels are active year-round; summer's snakes and lizards prefer warm days to cool ones; and the black-and-white aerialists with cigar-shaped bodies and a *screee screeee* call are all white-throated swifts, hoovering up high-flying insects. Summer also brings out the western bluebirds, rusty-red below, blue above, and fly-catching attractively under the pines. The trees themselves are tall and varied. My field journal from a recent visit notes: "Coulter pine, sugar pine, ponderosa, incense cedar, Douglas fir, oaks, snapdragons, milkweed, and penstemons." (I also have a grumpy footnote about picking up three soda cans, some tissues, and an empty packet of cigarettes.)

    One strange piece of infrastructure zigzags among the buildings, as if each one is connected to the other by aboveground plumbing. These pipes do not carry water, sewage, steam, heating oil, or even air. They just carry starlight, gathered from secondary mirrors and sent in a vacuum to the main telescope where it is collated into a brighter, more intense nighttime image. Supposedly, if you hold a seashell to your ear, you can hear the ocean. If you laid your head against these pipes, would you hear the rest of the universe?

▴ Western whiptail is also called tiger whiptail. It eats crickets and spiders.

Our home neighborhood, the Milky Way Galaxy, is one of 100 billion galaxies in the universe. ▸

KELSO DUNES
MOJAVE NATIONAL PRESERVE

"Booming" dunes—giant sand dunes that make a tuba-like reverberation

DIFFICULTY
Moderate to Hard

LOCATION
Kelso Dunes Road off Kelbaker Road

LENGTH
2 to 3 miles

Wind makes sand dunes sing—we all can think of a sci-fi or Foreign Legion movie with a rising whine of sound as a dust cloud nears—but only a few dune complexes in the world will boom deep and long when you walk on them. Kelso is one.

The boom is a deep hum or vibration, described as roaring, rumbling, moaning . . . or booming. The Park Service says this: "It's a deep, eerie, rumbling sound you can feel in your bones; a rumbling vibration through your entire body. The best way to hear the booming is to have a big group all on the crest at the same time trying to shove off as much sand as possible, like an avalanche. Visitors will have more luck with this if they are on a crest no one has walked on recently." A more technical paper fine-tunes the description, saying the "sound has a dominant audible frequency (70–105 Hz) and several higher harmonics and may be heard from far distances away. A natural or induced avalanche from a slip face of the booming dune triggers the emission that may last for several minutes."

‹ Kelso Dunes rise 600 feet above the desert floor.

The train station at Kelso Depot is now the regional visitor center. ▾

This emission *probably* happens—and nobody is entirely sure—because large dunes are not uniform. They are made up of layers of sand of differing density and wetness, and these layers can stay intact even as dunes slowly migrate across the landscape. If the dune is large

Moonlight and star trails combine to create
a subtle, pastel light.

enough and the boundary levels sheer enough, and if the sand has x amount of quartz of y grain size at z moisture level, then one layer of sand interacting with another layer causes the entire dune to resonate.

Or to be more direct, in the words of one ten-year-old visitor, "If you jump off the top really hard, it makes the sand fart."

The dunes come from sand in ancient lake beds that has been picked up by the wind—wind that roars and flows, eddies and stalls, just like water in a turbulent river. Due to the shape of local passes, all that sand ends up here. Only a small amount comes on each gust, but added up over thousands of years, the dunes can reach tall heights. National Park Service once more: "Winter and summer bring predominant winds from different directions, so the shapes and patterns of individual dunes varies daily and seasonally, but the dune field as a whole is stable. At Kelso Dunes, crests travel back and forth within a zone of 30–40 feet wide, like sea waves."

From the parking lot, the trail starts out centralized and obvious, but once in loose sand, paths vary, depending on which ridgeline people decide to follow. Some visitors find the hike more strenuous than others, depending how you feel about the "two steps forward, one step back" reality of walking in steep sand. Luckily the views are equally good everywhere in the dune complex, so you can't go wrong. Winter visits can even offer panoramas that include touches of snow on the nearest mountains.

While they look desolate, sand dunes are productive habitats just the same as tide pools or the mossy canopy of a tropical rain forest. Deserts offer opportunities and also challenges, just as all ecologies do. For instance, dunes offer a lot of unimpeded sunlight, which is good if you are a creosote or a chilly lizard on a spring morning, but it is bad if your taproot can't find a water source. Dunes create great thermals if you're a turkey vulture or migrating hawk, making it easy to kettle up higher and higher without flapping once. Too bad there are not any dead deer or stillborn calves to feed on. From a hawk's perspective, annoyingly, even Kelso's snakes know how to stay out of sight.

Two special animals to watch for here are both lizards. Midsized and easy to see when basking (and very hard to spot when under bushes), leopard lizards are agile jumpers and fast runners. They are famous for being able to run on their rear limbs for short distances.

They usually hunt in the morning and hide in shade during the heat of the day. Females (such as the one shown below) develop reddish-orange spots to show they are ready to mate; the colors fade after the eggs are laid.

Leopard lizards are named for their spots, which help them hide in dappled shade. ▾

Fringe-toed lizards can be found throughout the Mojave National Preserve, but they are particularly common around Kelso Dunes. Tan above, white below, this lizard has a back that is densely speckled by red and black rosettes. The throat's black boomerang pattern breaks

up its silhouette as it looks over the top of a dune or out from its hole, and the tail ends in white and black stripes to help distract would-be predators. Besides the usual lizard preference for beetles, crickets, and spiders, these lizards will also eat bees, mice, and even small snakes. More surprisingly, they are omnivorous and eat plants, including leaves, berries, and flowers.

The common name comes from special scales on the toes that form a fringe, which increases the surface area and allows them to run lickety-split across the sand without sinking in. The extended toes have been compared to snowshoes, but if so, these are jet-assisted snowshoes. As one field guide points out, "With their extreme camouflage and lightning-fast speed, getting a good look at a fringe-toed lizard is the novice herpetologist's holy grail."

We wish you luck on that quest (and all the others in this book).

BIG MORONGO CANYON

SAND TO SNOW NATIONAL MONUMENT

*Green trees and red flycatchers
in a lush desert oasis*

DIFFICULTY
Easy to
moderate

LOCATION
Highway 62, in the town of Morongo Valley

LENGTH
1 to 8 miles

Come for the bird-watching, stay for the hiking—or is it the other way around? Birders know Morongo as *the* place in California to see the vermilion flycatcher as well as 240 other species of birds. Black-masked, black-winged, and electric scarlet everywhere else, the vermilion flycatcher is the kind of bird that makes even the most die-hard non-bird-watcher perk up and take notice. It is so bright that it's very easy to spot, but it does have to compete for your attention with the variety of the lush vegetation. Filled with cottonwoods and four species of willow, Morongo Canyon is one of the ten best riparian forests left in California.

‹ Mature cotton-woods provide cool shade for summer hikes.

A cement puma on the roof of the education center reminds us to be alert for the real thing. ▾

Walks start at the entrance kiosk and can go as far as 8 miles round-trip. On a first visit, try the Marsh Trail, going left from the entrance. When you get to the education center (which has a discon-certingly lifelike cement puma on the roof), continue on the half-mile

loop of the Mesquite Trail. A water drip at the education center attracts white-winged doves, Gambel's quail, California thrash-ers, and migrating warblers; the adjacent palm trees might have hooded orioles. The preserve is closed after dark, which means there's no chance to get the coolest shot of all: a photo of a real mountain lion up on the roof next to the fake one.

The longest hike in the preserve continues downcanyon from the educa-tion center and is an out-and-back on the Canyon Trail. People have seen bighorn sheep here, so maybe you will, too. It can be hot and sunny on this trail in the warm months—so a hat and water are always suggested.

Besides the flycatcher, another all-red bird in summer is the well-named summer

tanager, so if you have binoculars, do bring them, even if you're mostly here to hike. You may also want your smart phone. Spring mornings often mean competing torrents of birdsong. Phone apps that can ID birds by sound are increasingly popular, though knowing which vireo is singing and being able to spot it in the trees are two different things. Hawks, wrens, woodpeckers: more or less any page of the bird book you turn to, something on it will be possible here. Organized bird walks can help novices learn avifauna with experienced guides, or just asking anybody else, "Hey, what's that?" can get good answers, or at least find somebody to commiserate with over the baffling frustration of all LBJs—"little brown jobs," the birder term for the multitude of small brown species.

▲ The vermilion flycatcher is a preserve specialty.

Cottonwood trees mean water, as do flowers like yerba mansa, which can form dense carpets around the wetter parts of the preserve. Yet this is a desert otherwise, and the preserve is not far from the world-famous Joshua Tree National Park. What brings so much water to the surface?

The short answer is earthquakes, or at least earthquake fault lines. The Morongo Valley Fault runs through the canyon—or to put it another way, the canyon follows and makes visible the main fault. Melting snow from the surrounding San Bernardino Mountains percolates into the sandy soil as it crosses the Morongo Basin, staying underground. But as the groundwater enters Big Morongo Canyon, it encounters "fault gouge" (pulverized rock), which forces the water above the ground, creating a unique desert wetland with a series of perennial springs. The creek intermittently rises to the surface for just 3 miles before it disappears underground again. Water in the desert: rare but logical.

▴ The white blossom of yerba mansa lights up a wet meadow.

Ancient rock rises up here. Big Morongo Canyon has some of the oldest exposed rocks in California, at about two billion years old. They include granite that has been altered by centuries of heat and pressure to form gneiss and schist.

Human history in the canyon follows the usual trajectory: Native Americans, Anglo-European settlers, ranches of varying sizes and varying degrees of success, and then from 1968 until now, the slow accumulation of land set aside for conservation and transferred to public management. In 2016, Big Morongo Canyon Preserve became part of the Sand to Snow National Monument and now encompasses 31,000 acres, with wildlife

▴ Cottonwoods turn yellow in fall and drop their leaves, which linger for months beside the trails.

corridors connecting the preserve with the Joshua Tree National Park. These routes explain why you might run into a sign warning of recent bear sightings, or why, if you're first on the Marsh Trail in the morning, you can expect to step over scat piles where the raccoons have marked sections of boardwalk as their exclusive territory. (All of Morongo belongs to raccoons: they just loan it to us in the daytime when they don't need it anymore.)

If you don't encounter a vermilion flycatcher in the main preserve, it also can be seen in the abandoned fields between the entrance kiosk and Covington Park, or even in the park itself, flycatching from the swings. Like its relatives the black phoebe and the Say's phoebe, the vermilion flycatcher typically waits on a perch, scans around, and sallies out after moths and large insects. It is not very patient; after a few minutes, if it has no luck, it moves on. That's often how you can first spot it, and then you can zoom in once it settles down on a new branch or fencepost. The picture on page 156 was taken right from the parking lot—once you know the trick to finding them, vermilion flycatchers become one of the greatest birds ever.

SILVERWOOD WILDLIFE SANCTUARY

DIFFICULTY
Easy

More than 300 native plants in a compact sample of pristine chaparral

LENGTH
1 to 3 miles

LOCATION
Wildcat Canyon Road between El Cajon Mountain Trailhead and the Barona Indian Reservation

Rocks, sky, and chaparral—the quintessential Southern California ecosystem.

Because Silverwood is a San Diego Audubon site run by volunteers, it is open fewer days per week than most other parks in this book. And at 785 acres, compared to the other sites, it may be smaller as well. Yet for texture and color, it is a botanical gem, and all the plants here are native to California, with many limited to this exact habitat, which one might label "post-burn upland coastal chaparral." That means these are tough, fire-adapted, drought-tolerant plants, sometimes drab or shut down in the dry season, but ready to splash out bright colors when it's time to bloom. And whenever you have an intact botanical community, everything else also flourishes, so this sanctuary is good for spotted towhees, Anna's hummingbirds, and Bewick's wrens, for titmice and bushtits, owls and orioles. It would be impossible to visit and not see *something*.

From the entrance, take a main, central trail straight into the heart of the preserve, paralleling the dirt access road and stopping to read the labels on the plants. A quick detour onto the ethnobotany loop takes you back onto the central path. When the trail ends in half a mile at the manager's residence, bird feeders, and picnic tables, the Chaparral Trail lifts you up into the hillside before circling back to the feeders. Other options are available, too; see the online trail map to connect short loops and cover 5 miles or more.

The word "chaparral" comes originally from Spanish words that meant a cluster of small oaks, and as a plant community it can indeed include scrub oak, *Quercus berberidifolia*. More typically we think not of trees but of large, hard-leaved, summer-dormant shrubs, plants which can create a canopy 10 to 20 feet tall. That includes the native but problematic poison

Scarlet larkspur is usually 2 or 3 feet tall but can grow to 6 feet. ▸

Poison oak turns red in summer and fall. Leaves come in clusters of three—hence the rhyme, "leaves of three, leave it be." ▾

‹ Fierce looking but safe to touch, this is the dried seedpod of wild cucumber.

oak, a vine or shrub whose berries can feed birds and mammals alike, but whose red-tinged leaves bring out a burning rash in most humans. Manzanita is here, with red trunks and small, flat, oval leaves, and the southern bush monkeyflower, with a showy yellow blossom that to some creative dreamers looks like a scrunched-up monkey's face. Sugar bush (also called sugar sumac) has pink flowers and small red fruits that can be eaten raw, used to make a tart drink, or dried and stored for later. They favor slopes, even the hotter south-facing ones, and so help stabilize the soil. Sugar bush shares one characteristic with almost all chaparral plants: after a fire it often grows back quickly, either from its root crown or from seeds that have been waiting for the heat of a passing fire in order to "know" it's time to germinate. Fire opens up access to sunlight for young plants and returns essential minerals to the soil.

Dodder is a sprawling parasite that some people think looks like a children's toy called Silly String. After germinating from a seed in the ground (the mature plant produces pea-sized fruits), it uses chemical clues to "sniff out" a host plant, which it clings

A tangle of parasitic dodder drapes across a laurel sumac. Dodder is also called spaghetti weed and witch's hair. ▸

to, penetrates, and slowly ascends up and across. Along the way it abandons the root stem and lives off the victim plant, penetrating the host's vascular system and potentially weakening it so much the host dies. No matter, since by then the dodder may already have reached out and draped itself across a neighboring bush.

There are many dodder species in North America, and as this photo shows, it is a normal part of the ecosystem. Once you learn to watch for it, you will spot it in plant communities around the state. (Since it is bright orange, you can even identify it from the freeway.)

At Christmas, we kiss under mistletoe, which is another parasite, often on sycamores and other "nice" trees. In conversational English, we condemn somebody for being a parasite, but if the goal of any plant is to find a reliable energy source and then pass on offspring, dodder's lifestyle makes perfect sense. In the case of mistletoe, it spreads easily because its fruit is deeply attractive to a native bird, the phainopepla, which swallows the mistletoe berries whole. A single bird can eat up to a thousand berries in one afternoon. After digesting the fruit, in just a few minutes the phainopepla poos out the sticky, undigested seeds, pasting them onto a new branch with a special dose of fertilizer. The plant then grows from there, infecting a new host.

Next Christmas, be sure to share that illuminating story with party guests. On the other hand—maybe don't.

BORREGO PALM CANYON

ANZA-BORREGO DESERT STATE PARK

An attractive round-trip hike to a native palm grove, with a chance to see desert bighorn sheep

DIFFICULTY
Easy

LOCATION
Borrego Palm Canyon Trailhead is just past the state park campground, near Borrego Springs

LENGTH
3 miles

Anza-Borrego is San Diego's amazing (and amazingly varied) desert park. By car it is just a few hours from the coast but seems to be worlds away in its stark beauty and many desert habitats. At more than 900 square miles, Anza-Borrego is nearly the size of Yosemite National Park. Some years it offers superblooms of wildflowers, though if so, also be ready for superblooms of traffic. In non-flower years, park activities include hiking, birding, herping, jeeping, horseback riding, and just about everything else except spelunking and scuba diving.

The state park's name combines history with nature. Juan Bautista de Anza Bezerra Nieto led overland expeditions from Mexico into Alta California in the 1770s. He later became governor of the Spanish province of New Mexico. Trails, towns, schools, parks, and golf courses are named after him. Meanwhile, in Spanish, borrego means "sheep," a term that includes the native desert bighorn, which are still found here. The Borrego Palm Canyon trail is a good place to seek them out.

The starting point is the resort town of Borrego Springs. Just south of the main village are creosote-dotted plains filled with freestanding metal sculptures of dinosaurs—fun and photogenic, if a bit startling the first time you encounter them. Borrego Springs also sees the annual arrival of another kind of dinosaur, since large numbers of Swainson's hawks pass through each spring. This open-country raptor breeds in the Great Plains and Intermountain West. In winter it migrates all the way to South America, going down through Central America and along the Eastern Andes to Argentina. Then, after fattening up on grasshoppers, it turns around and flies all the way back again. The route maximizes the ability to ride thermals along mountain ridges, and flocks of thousands of hawks make the six-week journey, usually in stages of 120 miles per day. Spring migration peaks in mid-March; the spring route often includes birds overnighting in eucalyptus trees on a date farm near Borrego Springs. Nightly roosts can reach counts of many hundreds

◄ As they recover from an arson fire, the palms themselves are off-limits. The trail goes near them but not all the way into the central grove.

The stark contrast of light and shade
makes deserts especially photogenic

of hawks and another hundred or so turkey vultures. In the morning, as the sun warms the nearby mountains, they all take off and keep heading north.

Look for this hike's trailhead at the oasis at the bottom of the obvious canyon just out of town. From Palm Canyon Drive, you pass the park headquarters, enter the park, and follow the signs west and north to the trailhead, passing several campgrounds as you do so. The pond at the trailhead has year-round water, so in summer it has bats and ringtails drinking at night, and bighorn sheep drinking during the day—*sometimes*. There is natural water in the main canyon, so the bighorn do not always use this source. (They seem to

‹ ‹ The ocotillo has green leaves on tall stems that end in red flowers, but only when it has rained. Much of the year it looks dried out and dead.

‹ This bighorn displays a flehmen response, analyzing pheromones with its Jacobson's organ located above the roof of its mouth. There may be females nearby who have caught his interest.

come here more often in summer.) From the pond, the hiking trail goes upcanyon a mile and a half to an overlook near, but not in, the native palm grove. The trail used to go deeper up the canyon, but fire recovery plans ask people to stay out for now.

One plant that can be fun to see here is the ocotillo, whose name is pronounced the Spanish way, *oak-ah-tea-yoh*. In the dry season, it can look like a bouquet of dried sticks, but with winter or monsoon rain, the ocotillo produces tiny green leaves up and down each stem, capped by a jaunty red cluster of flowers at the very top. It can grow 20 feet tall or more. Folk names include candlewood and desert coral; hummingbirds love the flowers.

Desert bighorn are related to Rocky Mountain bighorn sheep, the kind that can climb slopes too steep for human rock climbers. This is the species where males headbutt each other with resounding crashes. Bighorn are all-tan and heavier bodied than mule deer, with a white "target" on their rumps. Males and females both grow horns, though dominant males have the largest racks. In Anza-Borrego, bighorn are not hunted by humans, but they do need to watch out for mountain lions, which is one reason they do not mind coming down to drink at the trailhead oasis. Anyplace with so many humans messing about and making noise is safer, on average, than the wild habitat of the upper canyon.

ROCK HILL TRAIL

SONNY BONO SALTON SEA NATIONAL WILDLIFE REFUGE

An easy out-and-back for a midwinter taste of the odd, beautiful, "made-by-mistake" Salton Sea

DIFFICULTY
Easy

LOCATION
Start at refuge headquarters on West Sinclair Road, west of Highway 111

LENGTH
2 miles

Sonny Bono was a mayor of Palm Springs, a member of Congress, an advocate for the Salton Sea, and an entertainer who was the other half of Sonny and Cher. He died skiing; the wildlife preservation community remembers his conservation legacy.

As for the Salton Sea itself, it can play many roles. Is it California's greatest ecological disaster? Whatever it is, it is huge: it is 15 miles wide and 35 miles long, which is more than ten times the size of the City of San Francisco. Large yet toxic in this case, since it is hypersaline and loaded with hazards like chromium, zinc, lead, and DDT. Maybe the Salton Sea deserves its postapocalyptic reputation after all.

Or in another view, "the Salton Sea, an artistic Mecca"—pun intended, since there is a town named Mecca here—a shimmering dreamscape full of surreal scenes and fascinating (if curmudgeonly) characters. In this perspective, it is a successor to Spiral Jetty in Utah and Burning Man in Nevada. There is some truth to this version as well, since over the years it has inspired work by Kim Stringfellow, Richard Misrach, and dozens of other fine art photographers.

The future of energy can be seen here, too. There is talk of mining lithium for the batteries of electric cars, and geothermal plants tap into underground sources of heat. Grand plans always seem on the verge of happening. The next big thing is just one patent application away.

But maybe the Salton Sea is none of those, and at its heart is an underappreciated birding gem, full of migrant birds, escaped flamingos, and visitors like the yellow-footed gull, a kind of desert seagull that arrives each summer from

◂ In winter, the trail passes a pond, which can be good for waterfowl.

Receding lake levels have stranded a former dock. Barnacles arrived at the Salton Sea during World War II on the hulls of Navy patrol boats. ▾

breeding colonies in Mexico. This is the only location in the United States where you can see it. The region has a collective bird total that goes past 400, and even the site of this small walk has accumulated a checklist of 278 species.

▲ Dawn rises over Rock Hill Trail, Salton Sea. What birds will be out today?

To understand the different personalities, we spin the clock back to the start of the twentieth century. Over millennia, there have been many lakes in the Salton Sink, which includes land that is below sea level. As with Mono Lake, water flows in but does not flow out. Those ancient lakes had long since dried up when a 1905 irrigation scheme had a big oops moment. There was an attempt to make side canals that started at the Colorado River. Headgates failed, and the entire Colorado River made a right turn. Instead of going to the Gulf of Mexico like usual, the river flooded into the Salton Sink. Day and night, the water flowed and flowed and flowed—for two full years. The Salton Sea was born.

Move ahead to the 1950s. After World War II, America was ready to recreate. The Salton Sea, with fishing, boating, yacht clubs,

The 1950s live on in these scrappy, "never say die" desert communities. ▸

and waterfront housing, was advertised as the poor man's Riviera. Developments had names like Sans Souci, "without worries." Worry came, like it or not. To flush salts out of the soil, Imperial Valley agriculture used a lot of water, and all that salty water ended up draining into the Salton Sea. As water evaporated, salinity levels rose. Worse, the water levels also rose. The Salton Sea was getting saltier yet larger, and the lakefront houses began to be not lakefront but lake sunk as water climbed higher and higher.

Then, in a reversal in the 1980s, by lining irrigation canals and taking other conservation measures, the inflow was reduced. The salinity was still soaring but the lake now was shrinking, and lakefront developments became landlocked and weed-choked. Most of the fish died, and in some years, tens of thousands of birds did, too, washing up on the beaches in fetid rows. The *Mad Max* era of the Salton Sea entered popular consciousness.

Despite these die-offs, so far the birds have endured. White pelicans, brown pelicans, eared grebes, western grebes, geese, ducks,

plovers, and sandpipers—between one and two million birds pour down the Pacific Flyway each year and end up wintering at the Salton Sea (and in some cases breeding as well). There are desert specialists here like the ground-nesting, out-in-daytime burrowing owl, and rare seabirds like frigatebirds and albatrosses. The author saw his first kit fox at the Salton Sea on the same morning he saw his first albino red-tailed hawk and his first blue-footed booby. (The hawk technically was leucistic—nearly pure white but with a pink tail and normal eyes.)

Guy McCaskie, a legend in California birding, has been doing surveys at the south end of the Salton Sea for more than 50 years. He

▲ A burrowing owl stares down a visitor near the headquarters. Look for it along road-side ditches.

▸ Two geese take off at sunrise.

routinely comes up with a hundred, even 120 bird species in a single morning. A "bad" day only gives up 90 species.

Some of those species can be seen midwinter from this level, out-and-back trail that starts at the refuge headquarters. Water levels vary; we hope on your visit you have a "birdy" day, full of geese, ducks, towhees, and snipe, but there is no guarantee what will be around, nor in what quantity.

EPILOGUE

‹ A migrating
warbler pauses in
a boer-bean tree in
the heart of urban
Los Angeles.

This book ends as it started, with a question about the glass-half-empty, glass-half-full reality of the environment today. Is your personal California the one of fires and floods, a disaster-filled dead zone where even the dreams feel a bit shabby, a bit past their sell-by date? Or do you want to be one of the people who looks at places like Death Valley, Sequoia, Lava Beds, and Point Reyes and thinks, "Wow, this is so cool—look at all this nature, *and it's all just for me.*"

In the several hundred separate ecologies we can identify in California, almost all are still there—we have not ruined nature, or made it stop existing. We have influenced it, surely, and we now have blends of species and mixtures of habitats, especially around our homes and towns. The Redding Arboretum is an example of that, or the town of Arcata up to and including what can be seen in the marsh and tidelands. Nature is not static, nor is it something that is binary. It is not true that it is either pure, virginal, and unsullied, or degraded and not worth visiting. That is much too simplistic. Over time, ecologies change, such that once-logged pastures can regrow to become redwood forests again, such as at the Kruse Rhododendron reserve north of Fort Ross. Abalone is now rare along the Monterey coastline. That is partly because of over-collecting by humans, but partly because abalone-eating sea otters are now so abundant. Species recovery plans do work, and animals find ways to thrive even in changing conditions. Condors are back at Redwood National Park; California puma numbers are at historic highs; and if out in the middle of the night, you can see coyotes right in downtown Hollywood.

Nature is all around us, varied and abundant, and it is not going away.

We are the lucky ones who get to know that, and who get to go out and appreciate the surprise and beauty of it every day.

ACKNOWLEDGMENTS

For advice, photos, and good company, the author would like to thank Pamela Anderson, Paul Carter, Carol Chambers, René Clark, Mike Guista, Jon Hall, John Haubrich, Abbey Hood, Amber Hood, Fred Hood, Lynn Horowitz, Mathew Jaffe, Michael Light, Roger Linfield, José Gabriel Martínez-Fonseca, Amber Melhouse, Vivek Menon, Christine Mugnolo, Zia Nisani, Bill Noble, Carolyn Purnell, Fiona Reid, Mike Richardson, Micah Riegner, Brian Spillane, Santi Tafarella, Ian Thompson, Erin Westeen, Jeanne Wirka, and Cal Yorke.

PHOTOGRAPHY CREDITS

All photographs are by the author, with the exception of the following:

Anderson (National Park Service) 79
Andrew Cattoir (National Park Service) 168 (right)
Dreamstime/Vorasate Ariyarattnahirun 94–95
Olin Feuerbacher (National Park Service) 96 (top)
Jacob W. Frank (National Park Service) 83
Brian Grogan (Library of Congress) 78
Ryan Hagerty (USFWS) 85
Neal Herbert (National Park Service) 11
John Haubrich 20, 65, 106 (both), 107
Fred Hood 104
M. Juran (National Park Service) 24 (bottom)
José Gabriel Martínez-Fonseca 12-13, 24 (top), 53, 72, 76, 84, 90,
    147, 148, 149, 150-151, 170, 172
Killdeer Studios, p. 188
Kurt Moses (National Park Service) 16
National Park Service (uncredited) 2, 21, 30, 36, 81, 94-95, 96 (bot-
    tom), 97, 99, 123, 174
Beth-Ann Ostrander (National Park Service) 119
Shutterstock/Zack Frank 97
Susanna Pershern (National Park Service) 137
Joe Suarez (National Park Service) 15, 108
Brad Sutton (National Park Service) 8
Shawn Thomas (National Park Service) 39

INDEX

Born in Los Angeles, *Charles Hood* has birded all 58 California counties, photographed all 21 California missions, and helped to add a new bird to the official California list (Hawaiian petrel, also called the ʻuaʻu). He has been a dish washer, factory worker, ski instructor, Fulbright scholar, bird guide in Africa, and an artist-in-residence in Antarctica. Charles is the co-author of two other Timber Press books: *Wild LA* and *Sea Turtles to Sidewinders: A Guide to the Most Fascinating Reptiles and Amphibians of the West*. He is working on a new book about nature at night. Recently retired, he lives in the Mojave Desert.